ALTAB ALI

DEFIANCE

There are four books.

Altab Ali
Life & Family

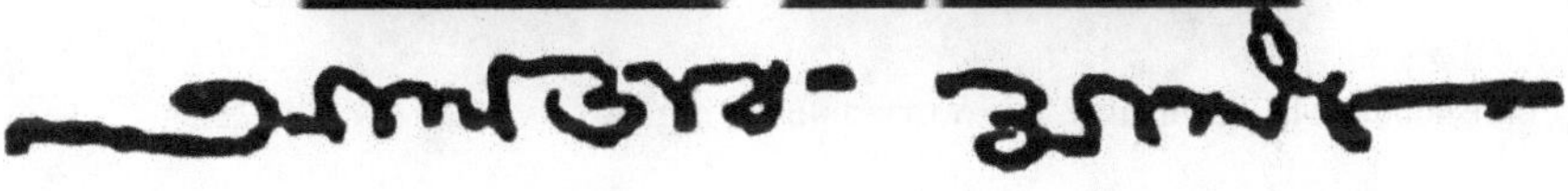

by Mayar Akash
Assisted by Ishak Hussain Akhter

MA Publisher

Copyright © Mayar Akash 2022
Compiled and written by Mayar Akash
Revised March 2023

Thank you to:
Julie Ann Akash for her support.
Ishak Hussain Akhter is Altab Ali's nephew, he has provided much of the personal images of Altab Ali and the rest of the family.

Published by MA Publishing, www.mapublisher.org.uk

ISBN-13: 978-1-910499-79-5

All rights reserved. No part of this publication may be reproduced, stored in a retrieval system, or transmitted, in any form or by any means, electronic, mechanical, photocopying, recording, public performances or otherwise, without prior written permission of the copyright holder, except for brief quotations embodied in critical articles or reviews.

Cover designed by Mayar Akash
Typeset in Times Roman

 Paper printed on is FSC Certified, lead free, acid free, buffered paper made from wood-based pulp. Our paper meets the ISO 9706 standard for permanent paper. As such, paper will last several hundred years when stored.

Dedication

I would like to dedicate this book to the family of Altab Ali who have lost a child and a breadwinner; they lost a son, he lost his life.

"And left his spirit for us to fight on."

I want to make dedication of the first and second generation elders of late and living for being the vanguard of our community in UK.

Special thank yous
To Altab's family members:

Abbas Ali, Altab's youngest sibling,
Hawarun, Altab's 2nd sibling
Halima Khatun, Altab's 4th sibling
Shitara his 5th sibling, the youngest sister
Ishak Hussain Akhter, Ukil Ali's son; Ukil is Altab's 3rd sibling.

They have co-operated in speaking with me and have expressed their concerns as well as their gratitude. They appreciate the fact that I want to portray Altab's life.

With their input the book offers depth to Altab's life, family and his world.

Special thank you to:

Ukil Ali &
Sheik Dobir Miah

Altab's bosom buddies who have also added depth from the East End side of London, UK.

Acknowledgement

I would like to thank the following people who have been involved in compiling this book.

Sheik Dobir Miah and Ukil Ali of Jogonath pur, Shamsuddin Shams, Jamal Hassan, Ansar Ahmed Ullah, Rajon Uddin Jalal, Ayub Ali Korom, Syed Mizan, Nuruddin Ahmed, Jainal Choudhury, Rofique Ullah, Jusna Begum and Shahagir Bakth Faruk.

I am also grateful and indebted to the following people for providing me with their support, accounts, time and energy in making this book bring this subject to life, and they are Ishak Hussain Akhter, Abbas Ali, Hawarun, Halima, Sitara, Sheikh Dobir Miah and Ukil Ali of Jogonath pur.

Finally and it would be a travesty from my part not to acknowledge the Altab Ali Foundation and Swadhinata Trust, Julie Begum and Ansar Ahmed Ullah, from whom I have sought information and support.

I would like to make a special acknowledgement to Renu Lutfa, for interviewing Abul Hussain in 1999 and capturing an insight into that night when he had to see his cousin's dead body, who sadly passed away himself not long after the interview.

Also Ishak Hussain Akhter, Altab's nephew who has provided from Bangladesh, verifications, interview transcripts of his family members, photos of the letters, wedding cards, passports etc. He has been the go-between for me in Bangladesh with his family and Altab's in-laws. Thank you so much.

The Bancroft library for their support and assistance.

Forewords

"Racism will never end as long as white cars are still using black tires."

"Racism will never end if people still use black to symbolise bad luck and WHITE for peace."

"Racism will never end if people still wear white clothes to weddings and black clothes to the funerals."

I haven't found the authentic source of this quotation but I saw some sources that claimed it's from Robert Mugabe the former president of Zimbabwe. Although it's a metaphoric presentation of racism. But; If we look at the quotation we can comprehend the conspicuous point of racism and it's root and ramification.

Racism is existing everywhere in the world little or huge. Even today we are being victims of racism sometimes in our country sometimes abroad. Bengali's reminiscences about racism was not joyful or isn't. If we look back to see the history of our ancestors then we can see the cachet of racism on their shoulders. They have unbearable memories. We have to remember the history of our ancestors.

When Mayar Akash expressed His, eagerness to write a book about martyrs Altab Ali who was murdered back in 1978 by racist attackers. As a family member of ALI's, I was very delighted by his scheme and I had assured him that I will help him by all means. I think and believe that only if we can spread the bloody history of our ancestors from generation to generation, then we will be able to establish our own Bengali entity.

This book is such kind of endeavour to pursue the history in order to transfer it to next generation. I wish the book continued success.

ISHAK HUSSAIN AKHTER
BSc. in computer science and engineering.
Hangzhou, China.

On 4th may 1978, our beloved brother Altab Ali who was murdered by racist attack at Alder street in London. From his death mourned the Bengali community that got angry which turned into revolution.

As a result of long movement by the Bengali community in 1994 the British Government renamed the St Mary's park to Altab Ali park. Today the name Altab Ali is a symbol of anti racist movement. More or less from that moment we all got to know about it.

However, people don't know much about Altab Ali as a person. He had left his newly married wife in Bangladesh and a loving family which consist of 10 members; this includes his wife, mother, six siblings uncle and aunt. Before he was murdered he went through many struggles in order to provide for his family; and after his death only the family knows the struggles they faced.

All these unknown facts have been revealed by the book "Altab Ali Life & family," which is written by Mayar Akash with the help of our family. He had taken an initiative to upload the story of Altab Ali and his family in front of public members.

My whole family and us siblings of Altab Ali are immensely happy and grateful to Mayar Akash. All our prayers are with him for the upcoming success for his future.

Altab Ali's family.

Contents

Dedication	5
Acknowledgement	6
Forewords	7
Introduction	11
Bangladesh	12
The Person	18
Star Signs -	21
Abdul Hashim	23
Coming To Uk	27
Bosom Buddy Ukil Ali	33
Living Quarters	38
Work History	40
Going Bangladesh	43
Sylheti Mindset	49
Socialising, Outgoing	52
Bosom Buddies	55
Moving In To Wentworth 1976	59
Wrestling	69
Abul Hussain	75
His Family In Bangladesh	77
Bringing His Wife Over	81
Altab & People	83
Time Line	87
Glossary	91
Bibliography	92
Source/References	93
Mapublisher Catalogue	97

Introduction

This is the 2nd book out of the four books written to be published. In this book I focus on the person himself and his family. I like to give a huge thank you to Sheik Dobir for his assistance and support in connecting me with Altab's family in Bangladesh. Much of the personal and in-depth information about the family has come direct from the family members. They were pleased to help and support me in putting this together, in particular Altab Ali's younger brother, Ukil Ali's son, Ishak Hussain. He was instrumental, he sent the images and pictures as well as arrange for me to speak to Altab's sisters.

Getting this information together is to humanise Altab Ali and share the true story of his life – the ten years that he was to live in the UK.

The insight in this book will also give you and show you how he was able to get over 5000 people to rally behind his mock coffin down to 10 Downing Street and Hyde Park. In particular the Bengali, Bangladeshi and Sylheti people.

You will find exclusive information about Altab Ali and his family, in particular his marriage and his wife. The timing of when all of this happened. You will need to read this book in conjunction with the first volume "Altab Ali Murder", which is how it is designed to be read, then the whole package will be completed with the third and final volume which due out the next year 2023.

Bangladesh

Altab Ali, son of Abdus Samad, was born in a middle class land owning family, 24.10.1953* in a village called, Mulla-Ata, Elamer Gaon, under Syedergaon Union, Burait Gaon Bazar, Chhatok, Shunamgoinj district of Sylhet, East Pakistan; six years after the British rule ended and partition of India in 1947.

Courtesy of Google maps

*date supplied by the family

Addus Samad his father was born around 1910 during the British Raj of India, he was one of four, he had a brother and two sisters. The younger brother of Altab Ali's dad was Abdul Hashim, who was born around 1917.

Abdus Samad's father's name was Faiz Ullah, he was the youngest of two, Faiz's older brother was Ziya Ullah.

Abdus Samad married Sunaban Bibi (from Bilfar, Gobindagoinj (Notun Bazar), Chhatak, Sunamgoinj) and they got married in 1947, and had the following children. 3 boys and 4 girls:

1. Altab Ali   b. 15.02.1953 - d. 04.05.1978

2. Newarun Nessa b. 00.00.0000 - d. 2018

3. Hawarun Begum

4. Ukil Ali
b. 15.02.1956 -

5. Halima Khatun b. 09.05.1961 -

6. Shitara Begum b. 15.01.1963 -

7. Abbas Ali   b. 05.05.1970 -

Abdus Samad died on 27th of April 1972. Shunaban Bibi was a widow soon after liberation war, she died of old age and ill health in 2008. The oldest sister after Altab Ali, Newarun Nesa died in 2018.

Family Tree

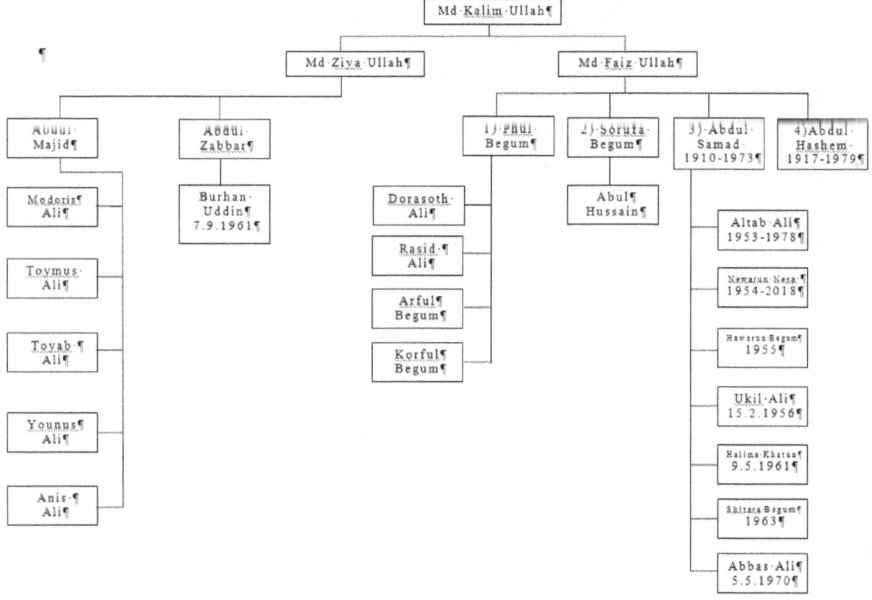

Information compiled and supplied by Ishak Hussain Akhter, son of Ukil Ali 16.04.2020

Altab's family reside in rural village and are part of a long lines of small land owners and farmers. They lived in a mud house supported by tinned roof. They primarily lived off their land but economic climate in East Pakistan was not very good, the British East India Company left their mark and then West Pakistan also siphoned out of East Pakistan. Living in East Pakistan was impoverished by famine, draught, flooding and lack of investment by West Pakistan. Thus leaving the people of the country in hardship and the people had to improvise.

Altab Ali was a child born free of British rule in East Pakistan and he would have been free of the slave mentality of his parents and many of the Sylhetis that were born before 1940 and those that came to UK pre 1947. These elders would have been born under British rule and would have operated in UK with the same slavery mindset. While Altab Ali was free of that mentality, his family were not, nor was his community in East Pakistan [Bangladesh] nor was the wider society there; it was a situation of "out of the frying pan and into the fire", the West Pakistani army treated the East Pakistanis with contempt, weaker, un-educated, fishing, fish eating, water people with hindu culture entwined. Like his father he was inherently sentenced to provide for the family, leaving little to their personal pleasure, leisure and wants.

The region he came from has seen deprivation for decades, high unemployment, high birth rates, tribal, and patriacal systems made it difficult adding to the historical fact of the British rule. Many thousands of Sylhetis have sought work with the British through the ships, as sailors, lascars; this was the main route to any employment, a low paying and dangerous one. He was fated to make this journey of his own, seeking to better his life and of his family.

This was his room.

Sitara took an oath of celibacy and has stayed in Altab's room. Here she is with his photo.

The Person

Education

It is clear that Altab Ali did go to school and learned Bangla up to his "Metric" similar to the then O' Level and today's GCSEs. He would follow suite like hundreds of other children living during that time. There is some fortitude here that he was allowed to study back then, this will be a foresight of the parents and grandparents. Having the vision for their blood to break through to the other side through education, enable them with the tools of reading and writing.

Altab Ali learned to read and write English in East Pakistan which would have given him much advantage over many elder Bangladeshis living in UK and other peers who did not attain much.

His primary school was Mulla Ata Government and his secondary was the Gobindaganj Bohumukhi High School; his college was Madan Mohan College which he didn't get to complete.

His family want to share with the world, the dictionary that Altab used when he was studying. He was definitely ambitious and was working towards fulfilling them, he embarked on couple of ideas and he saw one through with his friend but this did not go to plan

Altab was 5ft 8 inches tall.

Star signs -

Before delving further in to his life I wanted to include some of his astrological information to use as reference points and support understanding of Altab Ali's life because we are not able to get his firsthand account. All of this information will be collated through second person's perspective. Some information will be irrefutable such as his photo, his death, and his hand writing.

The following notes of what his date of birth reveals is here as reference to look into Altab Ali's personality and character and the accounts people give of him.

What did his star sign say about him?

Altab Ali date of birth is 15.2.1953, which makes him an Aquarius, Air sign.

He was a positive individual, who is approachable, responsive and masculine, his most important three characteristics were:
- Capable of manifesting own thoughts,
- Preferring to communicate directly,
- Thriving when surrounded by other people.

And his modality characteristics were:
- Has a great willpower
- Dislikes almost every change
-Prefers clear paths, rules and procedures

His Chinese animal is the Snake and he is Yin Water symbol,

his general peculiarities:
- Orientated to results person
- Efficient person
- Moral person
- Intelligent person
This sign shows trends in terms of behaviour in love which are:
- Requires time to open

- Dislikes betrayal
- Less individualistic
- Difficult to conquer

In terms of the qualities and characteristics that relate to the social and interpersonal skill are:
- Easily manage to attract new friends when the case
- Available to help whenever the case
- Very selective when choosing friends
- Seeks leadership position in a friendship or social group.

This sign comes with a few implications on someone's career behaviour:
- Should work on keeping own motivation over the time
- Has proven abilities to work under pressure
- Often perceived as hard worker
- Always seeking new challenges.

His personality descriptor charts rated 1-10:
Friendly: 3
Alert: 10
Diligent: 8
Active: 6
Tidy: 2
Prompt: 4
Popular: 9
Balanced: 2
Composed: 5
Sensitive: 7
Conscientious: 10
Consistent: 1
Materialistic: 3
High-spirited: 5

His luck features
Love: 9
Money: 5
Heath: 2
Family: 2
Friendship: 10

As an air sign he would be very jovial and lively and bubbly person to be around as he is naturally a positive person. As the water sign, inside he would be a soft person emotionally and would be an empath. He would make people feel good about themselves and make them feel appreciated.

Abdul Hashim
His Uncle

Abdul Hashim born in 1917, Altab's dad's younger brother had already been living in the UK from early as 1940s. He came over as a "British subject" on the ships as a lascar and made East End his home.

Abdul left his home in Bangladesh in 1932 at the age of 15/16 to seek employment like many others in the docks of Calcutta. He left without telling anyone, family or his village, there was no trace or news of him, nor did they learn that he had died from anyone. His family continued with life as best they could. His parents would have mourned inside, the loss of their younger child for over 10 years.

The family wasn't able to determine anything until Abdul Hashim wrote a letter to his family in 1943 from London, this would have had different effect, of relief, to closure from knowing that he was alive, and the ray of hope; because he was abroad.

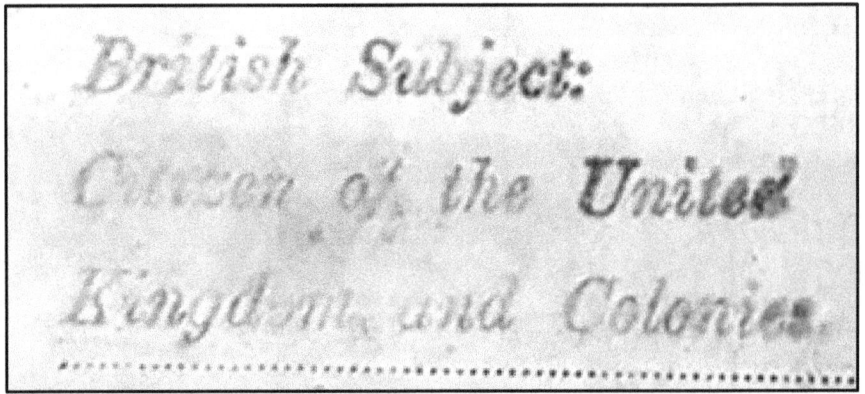

Abdul Hashim enjoyed the full benefits of having a British passport, from 1947 onwards.

Image supplied by family.

Few years later Abdul returned back home (India then) in 1947 (not clear whether before or after the independence. He was reunited with his family, while there he built their present day home and also saw his older brother, Altab's dad get married at the age of 34 years old. Abdul returned back to UK.

His next British passport was issued on the 15th of November 1957, expiring: 15th November 1967 from the foreign office in London. He was a British Subject: Citizen of the United Kingdom and Colonies.

During his life Abdul would have come and gone few times to his mother land, he lived through many changes and in particular lived through few nationalities; British subject, an Indian, an East Pakistani, and a Bangladeshi.

He became an uncle to many of his nieces and nephews as time went by, in particularly his eldest nephew Altab Ali; Altab was a good luck and a good omen for the family as a first born boy, very strong cultural belief of then and still exist today to some extent.

He then went back to East Pakistan to get married himself and on the 11th of October 1961 he had an arranged marriage with Johura Bibi.

Picture of Altab's aunt, Abdul Hasim's wife. Johura Bibi

Coming to UK

1968

Soon as Altab had reached fifteen in 1968 he came over to United Kingdom with two others Shomor Ali and Boshor Ali on the same flight on the 23rd of August

1968. They are likely to have gone straight over to Birmingham, Mosley where there would be work available. Where they will work and send the family money to support them, principle "Breadwinner". It is possible that they spent three years in the north, principally in Birmingham before they went to London.

His next passport was renewed in Liverpool on the 29th of March 1971 to 29th March 1981. This means that he had taken Altab Ali to Birmingham after they came to Briton in August 1968.

Here we have found records of Abdul Hashim's certificate in the National Archive, in conjunction with the 1957 Foreign office stamp.

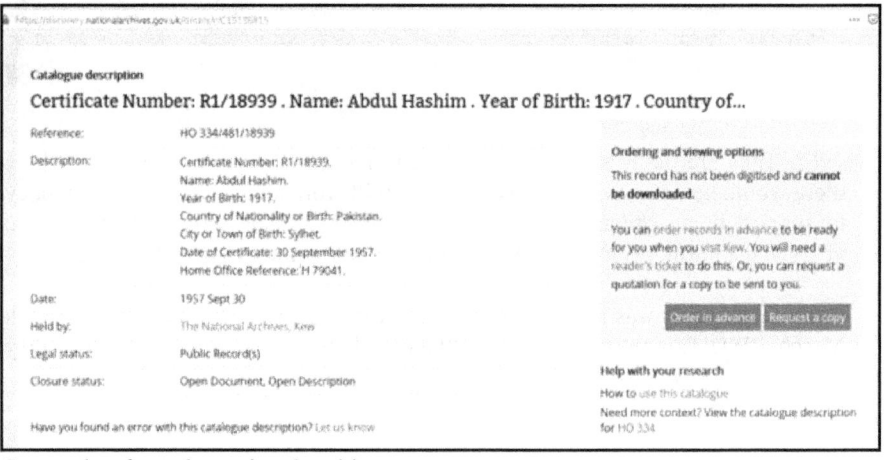

Screenshot from the national archive
Certificate number: R1/18939.

I have not been able to track down Shomor or Boshor, who can give some insight, word has it that Shomor Ali is aged and in ill health living somewhere in London.

[A point of note that the stamp reads "Dacca Airport Bangladesh" with the signature dated 23/8/1968. Officially Bangladesh didn't get their independence until 1971.]

In Spitalfields he was not alone, he had cousins already living in the East End and working there. Altab had five cousins from his dad's first cousin's side along with his uncle. He enjoyed the protection of his cousins Modoris Ali, Toybur Ali, Toymus Ali, Inus Ali and Abul Hussain who lived in Reardon house.

In 1970 trivia
> *1970 was the year that Concorde made its first supersonic flight, the Beatles announced they were splitting up and Brazil beat Italy 4-1 to win the World Cup. In the world of politics the Conservatives won the British General Election and Edward Heath moved into 10, Downing Street. The real drama, though, was in space. An oxygen tank exploded on the Apollo 13 spacecraft and concern for the fate of the three astronauts unified the world's population in a way seen neither before nor since.*
>
> https://www.wrestlingheritage.com/1970

In 5th of May 1970 Altab Ali would have been happy getting the news that he had an addition to his family, he had a baby brother Abbas Ali, their father's age was 60 years old.

16+ life
Altab Ali in his adolescent life grew up in this climate, from 1968 - 1978, when what was the height of "Paki Bashing" and the mental normalisation of an expectation of being attacked, being on your guard at all times, having eyes behind the back of your head was how people have been; he would have grown up knowing what the state of affair was in terms of the attacks that were taking place. Working in a factory has benefits, one of them is that all news will be discussed during the long haul of sewing.

Independence

In 1971 trivia
[Decimal coinage came into effect on D-day, the 15th February 1971 and wrestling fans mulled over why their 11/-6d ringside seats now cost 60np. Was this dumbing up? Notorious Haitian dictator Papa Doc died, the new state of Bangladesh came into being, and women gained the vote in Switzerland – but were still barred from pubs in certain parts of Australia.]

https://www.wrestlingheritage.com/1971

In 1971 Altab would have been involved with the issues developing in the motherland, the political unrests and the liberation war that was unfolding. All members of the East Pakistani community living in UK were financially contributing to Bangladesh whatever they could. Equally they were also physically taking part in the supporting of the events that were taking place in and around the United Kingdom and in particular in Central London; there were events taking place in Birmingham too.

During the liberation time there were small squirmishes* here in East London between the two factions in the community, the pro West Pakistani (the Rajakars) and the anti West Pakistanis, in and around Hessel Street and the surrounding Canon Street Road, E1.

He would have been in UK for over two years and be 18 years old when the independence war took place in East Pakistan for self rule from West Pakistan. Altab Ali would have been one of many fortunate ones who escaped the risk of being killed by the savages of war.

West Pakistani Flag

*Interview with Jainal Choudhury ex Tower Hamlet Councillor

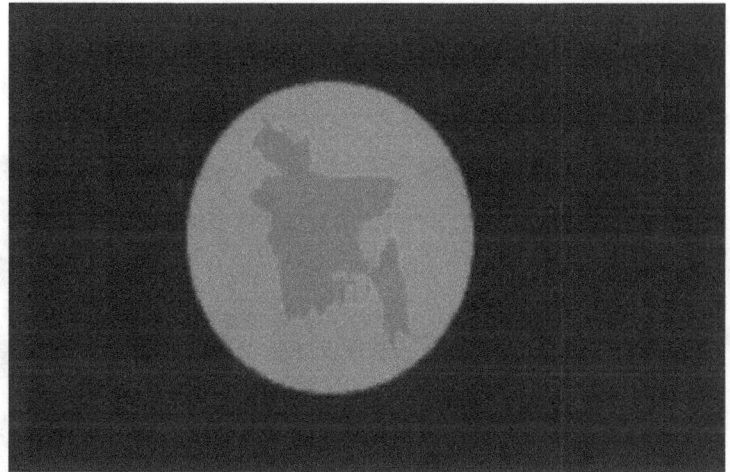

New Bangladeshi Flag

Once the news of the war was declared he would have had a sigh of relief like all others in foreign land, they're spared from fighting, yet duty bound to support the cause and country; as well as concerns about the safety and welfare of his family, his father, mother and six younger brothers and sisters.

In 1971 East Pakistan became "People's Republic of Bangladesh" (PRB). This is the flag used for the first two years 1971-72. He would have been glued to the news along with the rest of the Bengali community in UK.

Photo courtesy of the Londoni web site and Ferdous Rahman.

The pictures on previous page gives some indication of how many East Pakistanis were in United Kingdom in 1971, people would have travelled from all parts of the country to show solidarity at the event in Trafalgar Square in Central London.

[Photo courtesy of https://www.liberationwarmuseumbd.org/photo-gallery/]

If he didn't come to live in the United Kingdom, he would have struggled along with rest of the people of East Pakistan, treated as second to third class citizens with contempt from the West Pakistani Authority. He would have had to make a decision on which side he stood with "the East Pakistani Liberation Army or the West Pakistani Army, a.k.a The Rajakars". The Rajakars aided and abetted in the murder of the people of East Pakistan by the West Pakistani Army. Many. Rajakars betrayed their own clans and tribes.

So either way he would have been in the struggle of independence; he wouldn't of had the option but to fight for independence and get killed by the West Pakistani army.

On 26th of March 1971 Altab Ali would have shared the jubilation with the new Bangladeshi community on hearing the news of gaining Independence. There would have been celebration by the Bangladesh Welfare Association along with all dignitaries all over the country and then further jubilation of the surrender of the West Pakistani army in 16th of December 1971.

Bosom Buddy Ukil Ali

During 1971 Altab Ali met his first bosom friends by the name of Ukil Ali a.k.a M. A. Abdur Rahman of Jogonath pur, who used to live in Harris building and was a year younger then Altab, Ukil was born in 3.7.1954 and arrived in UK in September 1968.

Altab joined the factory Ukil was working in, ran by Suruj Ali who was also a spiritual singer known as "Baul Singer", who sung of devotion to god and godly acts, aspect of the sufi sect.

So, Altab was in good hands along with Suruj.

Altab was 18 and Ukil was 17, Altab would have made an impression on him. From that point onwards they bonded and were inseparable, they ensured that they caught up with each other every single day till 1977.

Altab and Ukil shared many experiences, they both clicked and became a duo, the enjoyed reading, watching wrestling, helping and various business ventures; partners in crime.

From the beginning of their friendship they both liked reading books, the books were not cheap nor readily available in London. They both shared the cost, chipped in and purchased books, took turns to read them. Sometimes one wouldn't have the money the other will cover the cost, and when they had the money they will square up, even if the other refused; they would put money in one another's pocket.

Altab's hobby was watching wrestling, he liked it so much that he use go to various venues to go and watch them, Altab & Ukil use to go to various town halls such as York hall, Shoreditch town halls and others.

Altab also used to do his own bit of social work, he use to read and write letters in Bengali for others and speak, write in English and understood reasonable English which he acquired in East Pakistan during his schooling syllables.

In 1972 trivia
> *1972 departures from Heathrow included Pakistan and Ceylon from the Commonwealth, whilst in this Silver Jubilee year of the Queen's marriage, her uncle the Duke of Windsor, the former King Edward VIII, died childless in Paris. Even if he hadn't abdicated, Elizabeth would still have become queen – just 20 years later, now in 1972.*
>
> _{https://www.wrestlingheritage.com/1972}

Entering into 1972 would have been a new world buzz with the dampener of the aftermath of the war, counting the dead and rebuilding of the country. Here in

UK the people of the new Republic of Bangladesh will have continued with their lives, working and making a living and supporting the country back home and in UK; the Bangladeshis with the added pressure of the racism they were facing in East London. This was a double edge sword, having gone through genocidel war and also battling here with the racist who don't want them here.

In 1972, on the 27th of April he would have received the bad news about the death of his father, which he may have been expecting as his father was elderly and with old age symptoms. His uncle already left for Bangladesh to be with his brother and also take his rightful place. When the time came Altab receives message from his uncle, that his brother passed away and his father is no more.

He would have gone through bereavement in UK away from his siblings and mum. He would have had the support of his cousins along with his friend, extended family, acquaintances as well as other village folks. He would have been mourning the loss of his father by performing namaz and reading the Quran, also giving alms. He would have also requested prayers be said in the mosque. He will have also been busy sending the family money to help with funeral and other customs, such as wake and further distribution of alms within forty days of death.

In 1973 trivia

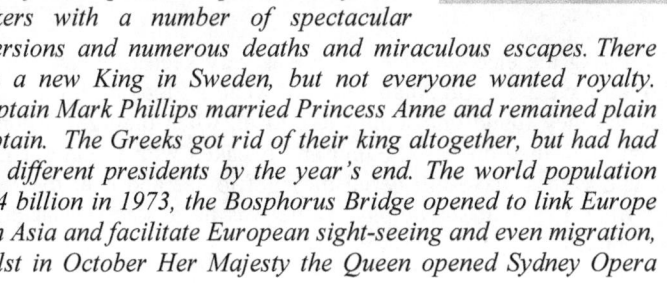

Edward Heath's Britain joined the Common Market at the start of the year. But these were the dark 1973 days of skyrocketing fuel prices, and wrestling fans were most affected by Power Cuts and the three-day working week at the end of the year. Meanwhile, the Vietnam War ended, the Cold War began and the Watergate Affair flared up. It was open season for hijackers with a number of spectacular diversions and numerous deaths and miraculous escapes. There was a new King in Sweden, but not everyone wanted royalty. Captain Mark Phillips married Princess Anne and remained plain Captain. The Greeks got rid of their king altogether, but had had two different presidents by the year's end. The world population hit 4 billion in 1973, the Bosphorus Bridge opened to link Europe with Asia and facilitate European sight-seeing and even migration, whilst in October Her Majesty the Queen opened Sydney Opera House.

https://www.wrestlingheritage.com/1973

This year Altab was in UK without his uncle and without a father. With a heavy heart he would do what he came over to do. To work and earn money and send it back home to support the family.

His social circle looks very tight from and his bonding with Ukil will have grown stronger and stronger.

Ukil mentioned that Altab liked the wrestler Dara Singh and all that I can find on-line that, Dara Singh was active in London in 1973 period. Dara Singh had matches in Southall and other places where there were Indians/Asians.

Wrestling Trivia
> *In the 1970s Tony and Gordon Corbett brought Lou Thesz and Dara Singh to Britain for three matches, with Tony refereeing on each occasion. Tony told us, "Although I had been wrestling for twenty years I was in the ring as referee and was completely mesmerised at the way these two legends applied holds and counter holds. A couple of times I was trying to work out how they applied a hold and escape and forgot to count. I don't think anyone noticed." Not surprisingly all three matches, at the Lyceum Ballroom in the Strand, Bradford and Southall, were complete sell outs. There was a near riot at Southall when Lou defeated Dara in front of thousands of his fans.*
>
> https://www.wrestlingheritage.co.uk/tony-scarlo

In 1974 trivia
> *Two General Elections saw close-run outcomes, both just enough for Harold Wilson to return to Downing Street. Edward Heath was in celebrated outgoing company as a number of world leaders came to a variety of sticky ends. Haile Selassie and Archbishop Makarios were deposed in Ethiopia and Cyprus respectively; the Irish, French and Argentine presidents all passed away, along with the prime minister of New Zealand; the Portuguese president resigned; President Nixon was impeached.*
>
> https://www.wrestlingheritage.com/1974

In 1974 during the election time Altab was very keen to watch the results but they did not have a TV. So Altab and Ukil went out looking for a TV and it just so happened they found one somewhere local, when they got it home it didn't work, that night they opened the unit and tweaked with it and got it to receive picture, and with a makeshift aerial they got to see and hear the results fuzzy "noise," what a spot of serendipity. Little was he to know what beholds him, what an irony?

It appears like what best friends do, they discussed, explored ideas and aspirations and many other things. It is clear that Altab Ali was an ambitious and a pragmatic man and together they both ventured out to get into business, they were entrepreneurs.

Altab Ali acquired knowledge of acquiring a licence to import bay leaf from Bangladesh. He must have heard or told, discussed this with people that he was working with, in the garment factory. So much so he got Ukil to commit.

They proceeded with the business venture and purchased a license for 20,000 taka. They progressed to getting the bay leafs and then it fell apart.

After the bay leaf venture fell through Altab was gearing for the next one, they spent time putting this together, all this happened before they went back home to get married. Altab identified that there was no petrol pump station in their area, he was on a winner there, but they didn't have the capacity to go ahead and materialise it.

Living Quarters

His paternal uncle Abdul Hashim accommodated him in the old quarters of the Flower and Dean dwellings, Josephine House.

Altab Ali enjoyed nine years of his life since he came to the UK, and six years of them as a Bangladeshi. He lived in Wapping, in Reardon House, Reardon Street, London E1, with his cousin and other relatives.

Carter House, Image from Google map, street view 2019

He was from 1976-77 living in a room in Wentworth Dwelling with Sheik Dobir and co.

He was living 126 Wentworth Dwelling, Goulston Street, London, E1 7PN. Infamous building of Jack the ripper's victim site.

During the time he spent with Ukil and lived in Wentworth dwellings, he was living near the skin heads haunt not far from where they lived. Ukil and Dobir have mentioned the Current affairs.

All rights belong to the image taker, Image from opensource

Ukil also mused about his experience with Altab Ali about the 1974 election and where they went searching the rubbish bins to find a thrown away TV. They found one and got that to work and watched the election coverage. What tenacity, practical, thinking out of the box man; on hearing this I was inspired; how resourceful he was.

artist impression

Work History

He worked in the "rag trade," as "piece work" in a factory based in 54 Hanbury Street, owned by Gulam Mostofa a prominent Sylheti individual who held various positions within the community in Spitalfields. He was also from the neighbouring village of Altab Ali called Toki Pur. It would have been incumbent

on him to provide work for Altab, because of patriarchy association; clan, tribal and neighbour.

It was hard grafting, physical and manual labour and long hours. The more you did the more you earned.

For a short while in 1977, he worked at 178 Brick Lane by the bridge, in a garment factory owned by Abdul Jolil. Roshid Jolil was a young boy who saw Altab Ali working in his father's factory.

From January of 1977 till 4.5.1978 his daily routine would be work home, [with the help of Google map we worked out his route, distance and how long it will take for an average person to commute by foot].

Gulam Mostofa

I just wanted to get an overview of the distance and a visualisation of it on the map. This map is different from the one that would have been for 1978. [we don't know the exact route]

This probably would have been his routine trip, he would be familiar and have confidence to walk alone home.

Not many of the workers had time to hung around as they had additional duties such as cooking and shopping, get home clean up and relax, recover for the next day, those days the wives and mothers were just arriving for many of the men that were working in the UK, until that point men were doing their own cooking and chores.

Altab Ali also made friends and one of them was Shamsuddin Shams, Shams was few years younger than Altab Ali, Shams was 18 when Altab was killed. They got to know each other because they worked in the same street, Altab worked at 54 Hanbury Street, and Shams at 64 and would cross each other's paths at least 3 times each day. According to Sham's they use to frequent the Sonar Bangla Café on Hanbury Street, they would socialise, keep up to date, watch TV and etcetera.

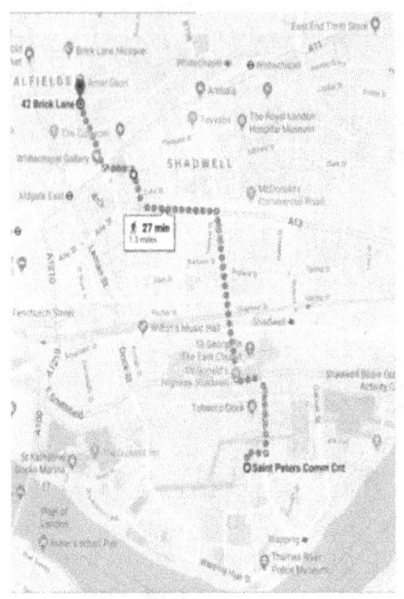

The bosom buddies were so closed that the talked, had discussions about getting married and spurring each other on as to who was going to get married before who and when. They decided that they would get married one after the other, irrespective of the order of marriage.

To think that the buddies had dreams, aspirations and plans to do so much together, after they got married they would be as couples together, socialise, meet and go out, invite each other to each other's home and etcetera. Beautiful seasons and life to look forward to.

Altab spent time talking about marriage to both his friends, with Ukil it was planning the weddings and with Dobir, Altab was teasing him to marry his sister-in-law. Quite clearly Altab liked Dobir and though he was worthy of marrying his sister-in-law to him, whether he meant it or it was banter it was a shared conversation that etched in to Dobir's mind and memory of his friend Altab Ali.

These are some of the thoughts Dobir remembers and muses, each time he bellowed out a deep sigh.

After Altab's father died in 1972, he was the oldest in the family and automatically bore the responsibility to become the bread winner of the family. This axed his priorities in place for him, he knew what came first. Work and earning money came first and everything else followed.

From speaking with three people of their firsthand account, Ukil Ali, Dobir Miah and Shams Uddin; Altab did socialise but very selectively. Shamsuddin's recollection of encounters with Altab was mainly around the work time, before, during lunch and after work. Shams met or saw him during lunch time catching a tea or grabbing a snack.

Altab enjoyed socialising after work, to relax, to take off the tension of a long days work and after Dobir was part of the same. Dobir met and saw a married Altab Ali, a settled, committed man with changed priorities in terms of relationship and women.

Going Bangladesh

Altab and Ukil made a pact that they will marry one after the other. So as they agreed Altab went to Bangladesh and got married and then returned to London and then Ukil went.

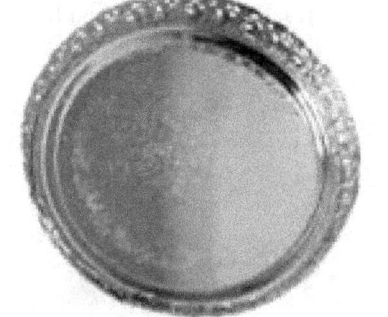

Going back to Bangladesh would have been a very exciting thought for him, this will be his first time in to the country. When he travelled over to United Kingdom with his uncle, it was East Pakistan. So much had happened since he came over in 1968.

All that killing and dying, the independence and the internal turmoil of the country. The country had changed, his father died, his brother was born, his uncle is now the head of the family; his brothers and sister have grown; his mother has become a widow and he missed them so much that he was going get to see them shortly, the anticipation.

He would have bought so much stuff for them and packed them in a big suitcase or a silver trunks, as they did then. He would have bought some jewellery and other items, one particular item that they use to take is the "fandan", beetlenut holders, made of silver or gold plated. An item of prestige for the community back home. Over in the village there is a lot of "fandanology, fandangry.

Since his father died he wasn't able to console his sibling and in particular his mum, so there are some closures that he will have; visit his father's grave and so on. He will also take stock of what he has contributed to, see what changes have been made and whatever else is needed firsthand.

There will have been some trepidation as he would have communicated to his mum and his uncle about the soughting of a bride and also planning. He would be reserved and on the same hand excited that he will marry someone.

Altab went to Bangladesh in 1974 and got married to his distant maternal cousin on the 28th of March 1975. He married his cousin Jahanara Begum who lived in nearby by village called Bilfar, coincidently his mother is from the Bilfar area too.

1975

Altab Ali's Wedding card

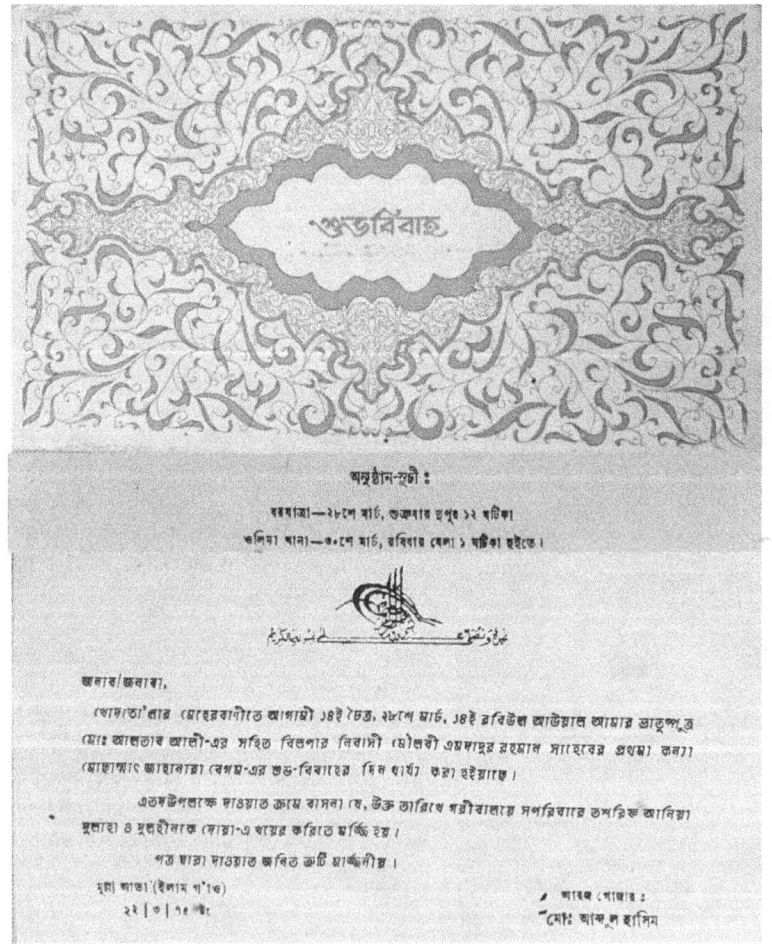

So in the card we have the details of the whole event, the wedding day on a Friday 28th of March 1975 and the Groom's reception known as the "Walima" was held couple days later on the 30th of March 1975 from 1pm.

His uncle Abdul Hashim was the RSVP, he was his guardian in the absence of his father who passed away 1972. Who would have thought that he would get married two years after his father had passed away.

After his wedding Altab Ali stayed in Bangladesh with his new bride for few months before returning back to Britain to continue to earn.

It looks like a humorous wedding gimmick, laid out like a certificate.
It would be consistent with Altab Ali's personality to have this certificate for humour

Here are pictures of Altab's father & Mother-in-laws Sufia Begum. His father-in-laws name was Moulavi Emdadul Rahman, he passed away 31st of December 2014. These pictures were from recent times.

After marriage Altab's father-in-law who is also Altab's distant uncle from the clan; he was a guardian figure for the family in Altab's absence. During his married life and after his death, he played a role.

Altab married their oldest child, daughter out of their eight children; they had 5 girls and 3 boys.

1. Jahanara Begum born in 13.6.1958, Gemini traits: extremely expressive, quick witted, sociable, communicative year of the earth dog, air sign

Altab Ali would have received so much love, care and attention from all his young in-laws as well as the same from his own siblings.

Altab's father-in-law became a bridge to a father now, Altab also became part of a another family forged through the marriage. We know from records and accounts that during the life of the marriage, Altab communicated through him and "care/of" him. We see this in the letters that he sent to his wife. It is a patriarchal custom to send it via the patriarch of the family.

The Wedding, Groom & Bride Shot!

This is my artist "computer aided design" (cad) impression of Sylheti wedding, images taken from photos supplied.

After Altab got married he stayed with his wife for another six months. He stayed with his wife on her whim.

He would have lapped up his new formed relationship and extended family. His wife had younger sibling, so they would have played about with him and vise versa. He would have enjoyed the receptions the brides side would have put for him.

Burhan Uddin, his cousin went with him to his in-laws whenever they visited, said by Burhan Uddin.

1975 August

In 1975 he got married and then return before 1976. During his stay Altab acquired some books about Sheikh Mujib.

Sheikh Mujibur Rahman, shortened as Sheikh Mujib or just Mujib, was a Bangladeshi politician and statesman. He is often called the father of Bengali nation. He served as the first President of Bangladesh and later as the Prime Minister of Bangladesh from 17 April 1971 until his assassination on 15 August 1975

Altab Ali was in the country when the assassination was unfolding in the capital city of Dhaka and he was in Sylhet his hometown. The gravity of the news would have spread like wild fire across the country.

Soon after Sheikh Mujib got killed there were lynching done on those who had book on Sheikh Mujib, in fearing that Altab Ali's mum discarded them books, recalled by Altab's younger sister Hawarun.

After the killing of Sheikh Mujib the country went through many changes, in coming government would ensure that there were no propaganda materials about and anyone found having any would meet punishment.

Living in Bangladesh is pay as you go and staying there after the wedding for few months were financially taxing, whatever money he took over would have diminished. It happens that he borrowed 5000 taka from his school master to pay for the return plane ticket. In one of the letter he wrote back home he outlines instructions to pay the school master his money from the funds he sent to them.

Altab lived in Bangladesh for a whole year, from December 1974 till January 1976; whole of 1975. 1975 was his merriment year where he was with his family and like all those who made this journey will know that and in particular the latter of them, that very few people will have returned back to Bangladesh to enjoy their life with their family.

Even Abdul Hashim, his uncle returned back to Bangladesh when the news of his brother was on his death bed; he stayed there and saw him through and stayed to take over the role of the head of the family; sadly he returned to UK to sort out his paperwork for pension month after burying Altab Ali; he died in the same hospital where his nephew was pronounced dead, the London Hospital, Whitechapel in January 1979.

Altab returned back to UK to resume his life in January 1976, now he had added duties to support an extra mouth, his wife's. He also now had his in-laws to acknowledge too, it was a matter of prestige.

Marriage
They were married from the 28th of March 1975 - 4th June 1978.

Altab Stayed on his wife's request for further six months, till January 1976. By then Altab would have used up all his finances and would have been compelled to return. We know he was short on cash as he repaid the local school master 5000 takas, which he borrowed to pay for the ticket and travel.

From January 1976 - 4.5.1978 - 7.30pm they were happily married and were working towards and planning their future life. We know form information we have, they were writing to each other and sending each other packages with local people and relations coming and going to Bangladesh. They were in love and committed to one another, sharing dreams and plans. Celebrated two birthdays and all the other traditions and customs, such as the Ramadan, Eids, shobebarath and other events.

Sylheti mindset

It is also said that Altab Ali was one of thousands of Sylhetis who arrived in the UK, to earn money and support the family back home. People of this category are not very exuberant spenders and will have had "hard graft" mentality and resourcefulness, and spend money wisely. They are duty bound, while they were abroad [in UK], their heart, mind and life would be in the village with their family; mum, aunts, uncles and the extended family. This was the "hallmark" of the early pioneers.

Altab Ali had gone to Bangladesh in December 1974 three years after the independence war and two years after his father's death; he would have been 22 years of age. He got married and did not have children from that marriage.

He has six siblings, two brothers and four

sisters, they all live in Bangladesh. They never came over to Britain, they are married with children and settled there.

In 1976 trivia

> Six years after its maiden flight the supersonic aircraft Concorde went into commercial service crossing the Atlantic in around three hours. In North America two young men started a company that was to become Apple Computers, and the Olympic Games were held in Montreal. Not that Europe didn't have excitement of its own. The Brotherhood of Man won the Eurovision Song Contest and in a non contest Harold Wilson resigned and handed the leadership of the Labour Party and Premiership of the United Kingdom to James Callaghan.
>
> https://www.wrestlingheritage.com/1976

After returning to East London from Bangladesh with a change of circumstance as well as having spent time with mother and the extended family would have quenched his longing for a while, but not for his wife.

Cultural & Customs

Now he would have another reason to work hard. Generally there is a large expense attached to weddings and being a "Bilati, Londoni," it is a house, to build a "Londoni House," back then it was an upgrade from a mud hut to a brick wall and tinned roof for some and for some a concreted block with many rooms like a cul-de-sac with tall boundary wall with iron gate (subject to land owned).

His priorities will have changed, he was providing. Altab had his life ahead of him, in-laws, children, the family gatherings, the celebrations of births, Eid festivals, observance of traditions, (Amm Katli, Mango & Jackfruit) giving and receiving.

[generally mango and jackfruit season are side by side, and in the season of harvest; it is traditional and customary to deliver some to sisters and daughter at their in-laws]

This tradition only applied to sister and daughters, after they are married off. This custom is a tradition and it is observed life long.

He would have extended his family in UK, and in-laws here would become family and the customary traditions will be fulfilled here.

Marriage was a big event in life, for him and his family. He will be looking forward to building his home, having children, building rapport with the in-laws. His parent will be expecting grand children, a social accomplishment, fulfilling of a cultural and religious duty, extension of the family, hosting and camaraderie, celebrations, what is inherent for many parents automatically.

They will grow old gracefully knowing that they were able to fulfil their requirements, expectation and societal initiation.

In 1977 trivia
> It was a grim year for Hollywood with the deceased numbering Groucho Marx, Elvis Presley, Charlie Chaplin, Bing Crosby, Howard Hawks, Joan Crawford and Rochester.
>
> https://www.wrestlingheritage.com/1977

Ukil went to Bangladesh in January 1977 and couple months later he got married, on 24th of April 1977.

Ukil recollected how both of them made mosquito nets for Ukil to take home, as these handmade were the best "mosquito nets." Altab also bought clothes for his family for Ukil to take with him and hand deliver them to his mother.

Unfortunately Ukil & Altab did not meet in good circumstance again and never got to embrace one another as they would have done if they met up in their ordinary circumstance.

Socialising, Outgoing

Excursions

Dobir stated that during the room share period of around a year, Altab and Dobir have done many activities as mentioned. He also said that when they went to see wrestling at the Royal Albert Hall, there was three of them, the third was Komla Miah, a work colleague from his Pakistani garment factory in Alley Street.

The below pictures are around Tower Bridge area, Dobir is in the white shirt and Altab is in the cardigan. He looks very hip and a trendy dude, [I'm sure Altab's motive was probably to send Dobir's photos to his wife to check his friend out for her sister].

It is becoming clear through this research that while living in the East End back then and being close-nit group, everyone acquaints with everyone [at least majority living in Spitalfields area] a common courtesy and respect. Majority people living and working in Spitalfields have same to similar story and the courtesy and acknowledgement is based on empathy.

Dobir provided these pictures that he discovered in his brief case, these pictures were taken by passersby with Altab's camera. Altab owned a camera!

There are factors inherent in this new close-nit community, their relationships based on family, clan, tribe, neighbour and who they grouped with when they arrived in UK, and naturally in the wider sense being the national, Sylhetis and then Bangladeshis. Further connection is through the same of everyone living in the borough, protection, self defence, they were victim of a common enemy, the fascists and the racists that despised them.

Acquaintances

So over time Altab had made acquaintances as well friends and bosom buddies. Acquaintances would be fairly large as he will have spent many hours with people in the garment factories he worked in as well as people he was crossing path with on a regular basis. It is a habit then to stop and greet one another and asked them where they are from in Bangladesh; and through this they will become familiar with one another.

Life before going to live with his cousin.

The outgoing man - Altab Ali enjoyed his life well with his friends, he was conscientious person, outgoing as well as homely person. According to friends' accounts he loved reading books as well as going to see wrestling. According to Ukil they went to various town halls to watch wrestling, this included Shoreditch, York Hall and Barking was quoted.

Both Ukil and Dobir have stated that Altab was an avid book reader, mainly Bengali books, he also kept an eye on the current affairs local and in Bangladesh.

Ukil and Dobir have both said that Altab loved wrestling and that they went to events with him. Ukil to the town halls and Dobir to the Albert hall, they both stated that he was a bubbly and fun loving person, he was very loyal and very selected close friends.

It is clear who his friends and bosom buddies were, people he lived with and shared his life with were his friends and those that he went further and socialised in excursions in to London town; there was some in particular he took a shine to and who accompanied him to these excursions, who he took photographs with and; referred to him in aspersion as his, "bairah", (brother-in-law, someone married to his wife's younger sister).

Confidence
Also the fact that they asked passerby to take their photograph implies that he or they were not shy or timid and were able to articulate in English a request to someone to take their photograph, in more than one location.

Liberated
It is also possible that Altab Ali felt liberated after getting married, he's the "Man" now and wanted to explore and show his wife his time in London.

Prayers
I asked Dobir if they prayed at home and he reply not really but attended Jumma prayers on Fridays in Brick Lane Mosque whenever possible.

It has been said by an associate that though they were not personal friends, "they", as country men working in the same area got together and spend their time socialising in the local cafes and in the local cinema at times convenient.

The café that they frequent was owned by a prominent Pakistani business man named Musa and one of many of his establishment was the "Clifton Restaurant," Other cafes they went to were Sonar Bangla Cafe and the "Naz" cinema and other surrounding establishments.

After work they would chill out in the café, discuss issues arising and old matters that are being dealt with. They have been to the cinema where they watched Indian and Bengali films that kept them in touch with the cultural sides of things.

Both Dobir and Ukil have accounted how Ukil and Altab walked to and from Barking at night without any trouble. Dobir also stated that after they returned from watching wrestling at the Royal Albert Hall, Altab and Komla Miah dropped Dobir off and then walked Komla to his place at Everard House and then he walked home on his own. This clearly illustrates that he wasn't a timid man or scared; he had his wits about.

During the time he spent with Ukil and lived in Wentworth dwelling, he was living near the skin heads haunt not far from where they lived. Ukil and Dobir have mentioned that they all had run-in and abuse hurled at them when passing the shop.

Bosom buddies

His time with Ukil Ali

Hawarun recalled Altab Ali speaking about his friend Ukil Ali, best friend from UK. Altab first met Ukil at Suruj's garment factory in Hanbury street around

1971 (according to Ukil Ali), where Altab went to learn sewing. There he was introduced to everyone as per normal and there, was one Ukil Ali, well that was a familiar name to Altab, that was his younger brother's name back home, and according to Hawarun's account, there was an instant bonding. They were inseparable until the time Altab went Bangladesh to get married.

They both were similar age, however Altab was a year older and it's most probably a reason why they bonded, probably because others were older - and in our cultural community especially, back then, age was factor in how you appropriate yourself with and around.

Ukil and Altab were avid book readers and shared the costs of purchasing the books and then reading them; mainly Bengali books and newspapers.

Ukil maintained contact with Altab's family and in particular with Altab's mum. According to Ukil he had been keeping contact with them and also assisting them wherever he could, that also included financial support. His commitment stop recently after Altab's mother passed away in mid 2000.

Ukil also has moved on from his old life, his life took a turn some time after Altab's death. Ukil turned to his faith and did away with all thing material and shed so much, including many person affect, including photos with Altab Ali; however, one survived; he believes that one of the children kept it, and that photo is the studio photo with Altab Ali which is featured in the book.

Ukil met Altab in 1971 and became very close, they were inseparable upon till the point Altab went to Bangladesh to get married; otherwise they did everything together, as bosom buddies do; they even discussed about marriage and who would get married first.

Circumstance didn't allow them to be at one another's wedding but they were in contact via letters. After Altab returned from Bangladesh in 1976, they spent few more months together before Ukil left for Bangladesh to get married in November 1976.

Altab had to move into another accommodation near where Ukil lived, Altab moved in to a one bedroom flat where his cousin was living with 5 other people, Altab will make the 6th. It is in this flat where he met his other bosom friend Dobir Miah.

We know from Dobir that Altab's association with Ukil did not stop then, Dobir said that it was a ritual to see one another every single day, either Ukil will pop in or Altab will pop into Ukil's to touch base. While that happened Altab got along with Dobir too, Dobir was younger than Ukil and with Altab's personality they bonded too.

Altab made sure that his friend Ukil to take some items to give to his new wife, mother and rest of his family. Ukil mused that they bought materials to make mosquito nets; the handmade ones were the best.

Ukil left for Bangladesh to get married saying goodbye to his friend, little did he know that is the last time he is going to see his bosom buddy alive; that this is his farewell. It was clear that they loved each other as buddies do.

They were going to meet again, they weren't to meet in Bangladesh for the happy occasion, their weddings but Ukil was going to receive Altab's dead body. Ukil his bosom buddy was going to be there to bury him, bosom buddy to the dying day and beyond.

Ukil retuned back to UK a month after he buried Altab but he didn't disconnect with the family. Ukil surrogated his links with Altab's family and maintained contact and assisted financially as best he was able, while looking after his own family.

Bosom Buddy Dobir Miah (Post marriage)

His friendship with Dobir Miah

They met after Altab got married, he moved into 126 Wentworth Building when they met, Shomor Ali, Altab's relative arranged for him to move in.
He became Dobir's roommate and they connected soon after.

Marriage proposition for Dobir
Altab was so happy with his wife and marriage and that he was offering his wife's younger sister-in-law for marriage to Dobir to marry. Wow, that is such an approval, Altab must have really liked Dobir, liked him as a person, good hearted and sincere and gentle person, otherwise no one would offer their family member to anyone.

Dobir, after Altab died things whittled back to life and back to the rat race. Striving to better one economical circumstance and also deal with the family, new responsibilities after getting married and then having children and so on.

Dobir's gone on to be a successful factory owner and played a prominent part just as Ukil who also had a factory. This kept their world ticking over and there was no interaction between Ukil and Dobir over the years.
It's only when decades on that Dobir came across photos that they took back in the days. Photos near Tower bridge with Altab Ali and their other friend Altap Miah.

This is when Dobir Miah was hit with a sense of obligation to find out about Altab's family. By then there are various initiatives that were keeping Altab's memory alive, there were, plays written about him, Altab Ali gate was installed and other fringe activities going on, but to Dobir's conscience, no one was really looking out for Altab's family.

Discovering those photos gave him credibility and not somebody jumping on the band wagon. He had proof of having links and connection with Altab Ali, he can now support and substantiate his claims.

With this he set out to find out more about the family and means to contact them. Dobir networked and warmed a group who were of same age and grew up in the 70s, who were around when Altab got killed, they were also pro-active through the struggle.

Dobir Miah with his personal expense went to Bangladesh to speak with the family. He was couple years out, he didn't get to speak or meet Altab's mum.
Dobir went over and spoke with the family and shared his thoughts and to understand, assess to see how the family needs support and how best they can facilitate this from UK.

Dobir got the family's consent in writing that they give permission and "power attorney" to Dobir Miah. In UK Dobir Miah became part of a collective known as the Altab Ali Trust, with this group and Altab's family permission to use their name and start to raise money for Altab's cause.

It appears that the "London eye," saw that they were still living in their old house and that hasn't changed; that they need a new house, so the fundraising would be for a new house. So the trust went about raising money for the house.

Dobir went to Bangladesh to hand over the money that the trust did various fundraising event on the Bangla satellite channels and raised over £9000.00. The money was raised for a house; however, there was a misunderstanding - this arose from, "getting lost in translation".

The family was not going to accept the money for building a house as that is what they didn't give consent for. And Dobir knowing that did not hand over the money to the family; because of accountability and his integrity, for him the money was raised for a house and nothing else, Dobir raised this money through the organisation and felt that he did not have the authority to hand over the money for any other reason.

So Dobir had an unsuccessful trip where he returned back to London with the dilemma. He had to put this to the committee before taking the next course of action.

Moving in to Wentworth 1976

Dobir Miah moved to this property in Oct/Nov 1975. Altab moved in to 126 Wentworth dwelling after his return from Bangladesh 1976, his brother-in-law Shomor Ali was already residing there. He shared the room with Sheikh Dobir and the house was shared among 6 people; Altab, Shomor Ali, Dobir Miah, Abdul Kadir the owner, Badsha Miah and Rohman Ali all in a one bedroom flat; with a sitting room.

Dobir Miah describes his time with Altab Ali, according to him Altab was bubbly and outgoing person but prudent. Altab Ali loved his tea, and Dobir went far to say that he was tea-aholic; he also used to smoke the all famous, red box with gold trimmings, Dunhill [I can recall seeing my cousin smoking Dunhill, the smell was strong in the late 70s]
They worked long hours, and him with his house mate will have gathered and entertain themselves while preparing a meal, they took turns to cook and eat together. Altab shared the one bedroom flat with a sitting room that was also the second bedroom. Altab liked reading Bengali books and newspapers, he also wrote letters to his family and wife.

Dobir recalls that Saturday was a wash run. Their flat did not have bathing facilities so they use to go to the local swimming baths and have their wash once a week. There use to be a long queue; about 20-30 people waiting to have a 30 minutes wash time.

They all got acquainted with the, what he describes an African janitor, who was responsible for the cleaning of the cubicles after each wash. After a while the Janitor was referred to as Abdul by them all and they interacted with him.

Abdul the janitor on the other hand use to charge each person 10p to clean the cubicle and refused if they didn't Dobir mused. The Saturday bathing would have been another meeting point for the guys, a social event.

He left his roommate in January 1977. He told Dobir he was sad to leave him and his housemates, companions, buddies and the freedom, he was obligated to move because his cousin pleaded; his cousin's family needed additional manpower support in a very racist and hostile location of the borough. Altab and Dobir spent 17/20 months living and sharing the same room and had established a good bond with each other and rest of the flat mates.

This picture of Altab Ali is in the cardigan and Dobir Miah in the white shirt, also present there on the day but not in the picture was Altab Miah.

In this picture Altab Ali looks a bit more aged, hair cut and clean shaven, also sports a belly. Since returning from Bangladesh and having the added responsibility of the wife must have been taking the toll. He must have been also relaxed about relationship after getting married, thus just letting go of the images, at this stage he is of 24 years old.

His outlook on life would shift him to another level, now that he is married he would have to live up to expectation as well as fulfilling his own aspirations, as all Bangladeshi men did then.

There were expectations from back home that he is a breadwinner and he supports a whole host of family members as well as his local village. To build a house, buy land, cattle, plot in the town or bazar to make and hire out shops to create income and so on. I can see him putting in the long shifts 11-12 hours, 6-7 days a week. Living with his cousin and sister-in-law, he was in a happy place, he was fed well.

He moved to Wapping January 1977, after his paternal cousin [Fufu toh Bai] from his aunts side asked him to move in as they were frightened to live there. His cousin offered him rent free and meals will be provided cooked by his cousin's wife [makes his cousin's wife, his sister-in-law (Bahbee)].

Back in those days a ground floor flat was 'unsafe and vulnerable', quite often the proverbial brick through the window would intimidate a family or worst still inflict serious injury. Altab Ali's relative like many others at the time felt safety in numbers so asked him to share his family home in the newly acquired council flat.

This image from 2019, Google map

Wapping was one of the heartland of cockneys and would have become accustomed with the local traditions of the [East Pakistani] Bangladeshi community and his peers. He would definitely have had received the social education from the community and the youths who were already there. He would have made bonds and become integral part of local dynamic with the Bengali community and its politics, culture and religion; he may have attended local education to learn English and take part in other activity.

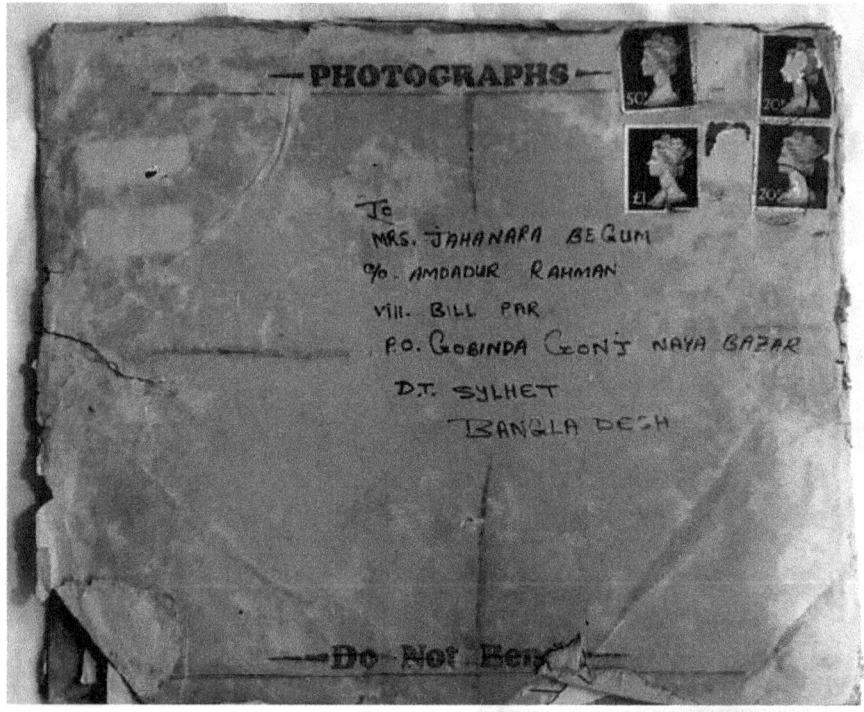

The family also have in their possession around twenty letters addressed to various members of the family, from his mother, to uncle, to wife, to cousins. They held onto everything they have and discovered.

This envelope is addressed to his wife c/o his father-in-law. The envelope marked "PHOTOGRAPHS," he was sending her some eye candy for sure. He had gone to a studio to have his photos taken.

We can see Altab's hand writing and that's how he wrote his wife's name.

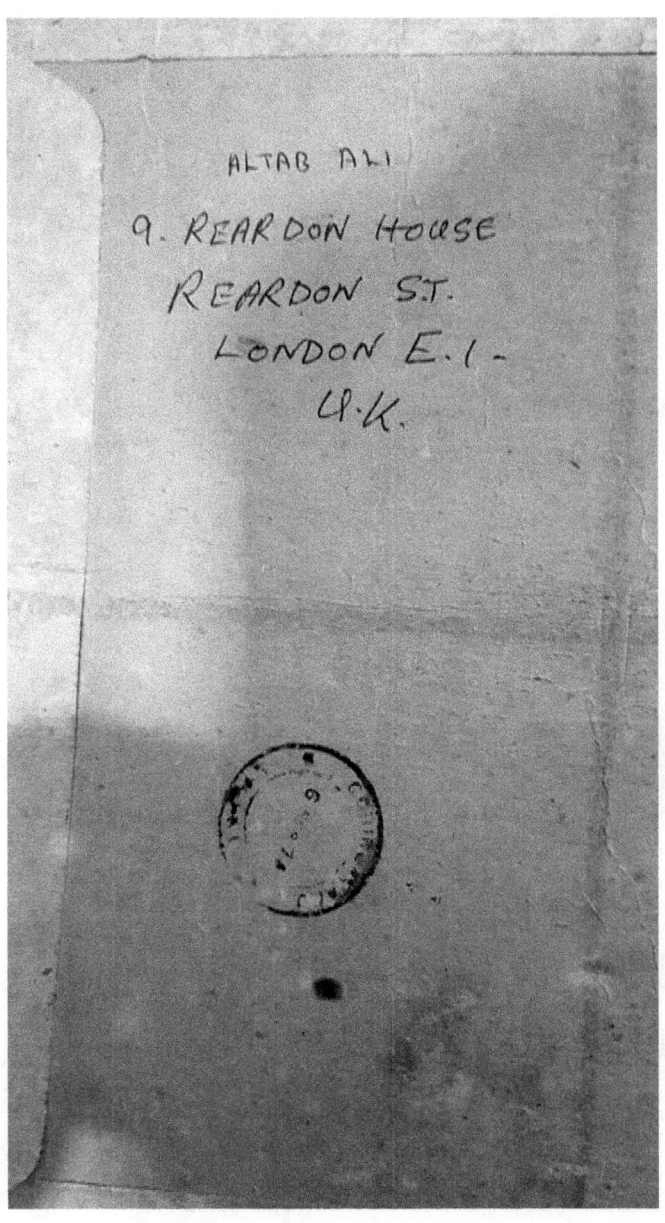

The stamp on the back of that envelope reads 6th September 1976, it contained the following photograph sent to his wife.

This was his confidence, smart and trendy appearance, just the kind of photo you'd send to your wife.

All these images and information is supplied by Altab's sibling and family.

This photo was taken after the wedding and before 6.9.1976.

These photos were taken in Whitechapel, Stuart Camera shop.

http://www.nobuyukitaguchi.com/en/about/[23-7-2020] This image is taken in 1981, 4 years after his death.

Incidentally, I had worked in this shop for 13 years on and off since 1991 for Mr Robert Stuart (Bob) and his family along with another Bangladeshi, Helal Uddin (H), Bob's adopted shop assistant son (lol)

Letter Dobir has kindly made this picture of a letter that Altab wrote to his family, it is stamped 12 Jul 76. Dobir was shown this by Altab's family in 2017 when he visited them on a humanitarian visit, in homage to Altab Ali his friend, Dobir felt that the family had been overlooked

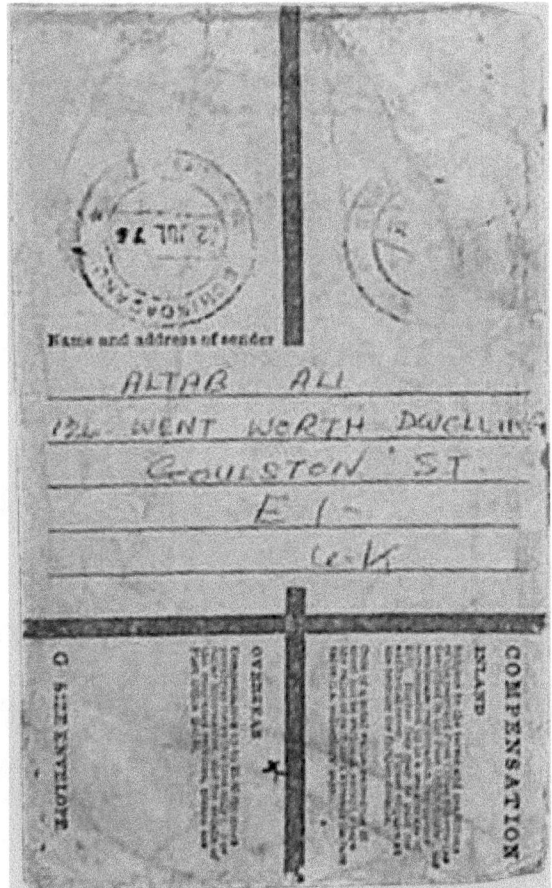

Altab Ali was educated in Bangladesh, here you can see his hand writing, he wrote the address in English, Dobir also said that his Bengali hand writing was equally good.

This letter would have been written soon after he returned from Bangladesh. This letter is treasured by his siblings.

His last letter was written on or before 3rd of May 1978 and the letter post marked on was the 3rd of May 1978; how would he know that his body will be received before the letter gets to them; in about 4 weeks from the point of posting. He got murdered on the 4th of May and his dead body was received on the 4th of June and buried on the same day, letter arrived after the burial.

During his life in UK he maintained communication with his family via letters. In them he would converse, tell them about his experiences and also give instructions as to how to distribute the money he sent to them.

These are just few samples out of twenty or so letters they hold dearly from Altab Ali.

Through these letters we can live through his life while living in the East End of Tower Hamlets. Through these letters we can also understand what kind of a person he actually was. [Bengali readers]

Copies of these letters were supplied by his sibling Abbas Ali.

In one of his letters he made known to his mother and his uncle that he was having a hard time in UK, work was scarce and wanted to bring his wife over to ease his burden of a man living without his wife.

These are some of Altab's possession that the family have held on.

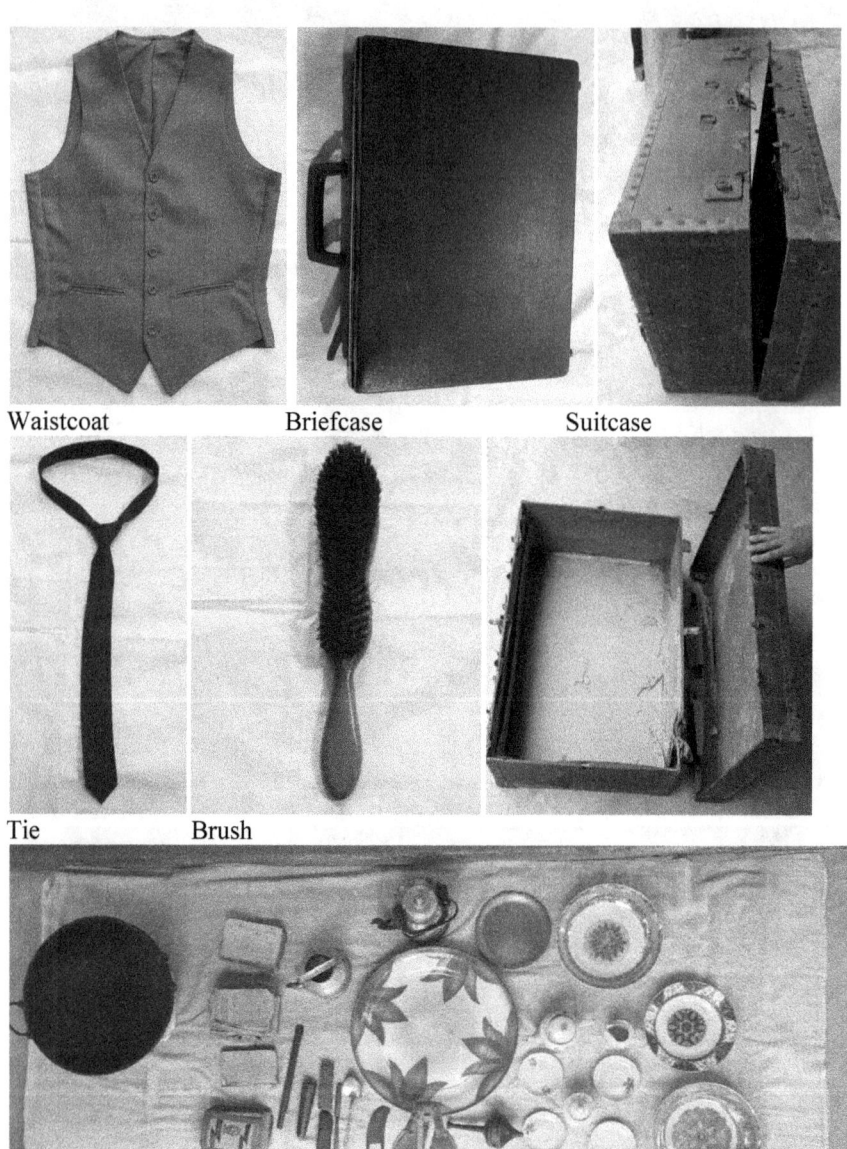

Waistcoat Briefcase Suitcase

Tie Brush

These are what is remaining from his wedding

Wrestling

Altab's personality and character
Further activities suggests Altab's like for Dobir, they went to cinema most Sunday to watch films, Indian and Bengali, at the Naz cinema in Brick Lane.

Altab also travelled to the city and visited the tourist spots such as Trafalgar Square, Tower Bridge, Piccadilly Circus and the Royal Albert hall to watch "Big Daddy" wrestle.

Altab Ali was an avid wrestling fan and in particular to "Big Daddy," even so he went to local events in and out of the borough, local town hall such as the York hall, Shoreditch Town Halls with his friend Ukil to watch local fights, he especially liked Dara Singh, India's wrestling champion.

In the 1970s Tony Scarlo and Gordon Corbett brought Lou Thesz and Dara Singh to Britain for three matches, with Tony refereeing on each occasion. Tony told us, "Although I had been wrestling for twenty years I was in the ring as referee and was completely mesmerised at the way these two legends applied holds and counter holds. A couple of times I was trying to work out how they applied a hold and escape and forgot to count. I don't think anyone noticed." Not surprisingly all three matches, at the Lyceum Ballroom in the Strand, Bradford and Southall, were complete sell outs. There was a near riot at Southall when Lou defeated Dara in front of thousands of his fans.

They freely travelled to these places and travelled back unharmed. Here is an account from Ukil himself, "they never feared to go to these events and locations."

Wrestling @ The Royal Albert Hall

On the 30th of March 1977 Altab Ali treated two of his friends to watch his favourite wrestler fight at the Royal Albert Hall. This may have been in celebration of his friend Ukil getting married in Bangladesh. His way of celebrating, raising his spirit.

Image courtesy of Richard Teubler @twitter

He took his roommate Dobir Miah and his best friend Ukil's cousin, Komla Miah, (Ukil was in Bangladesh getting ready to get married). They took bus trip down there.

![Wrestling poster - Dale Martin Promotions Ltd presents Wrestling at Royal Albert Hall, Wednesday 30 March 1977]

It was a shame that Big Daddy and Giant Haystacks lost but the crowd loved them.

https://www.ewrestlingnews.com/articles/the-best-of-british-vol-9-big-daddy-vs-giant-haystacks

https://shop.royalalberthall.com/collections/sport/products/pod1032773

https://twitter.com/memorialdevice/status/1225720129046052864

Giant Haystacks trying to take Kendo Nagasaki's mask off.

While they were there they enjoyed the line up of the event. Big Daddy's event was tag team, he teamed up with Giant Haystacks versus Kendo Nagasaki & Rex Strong.

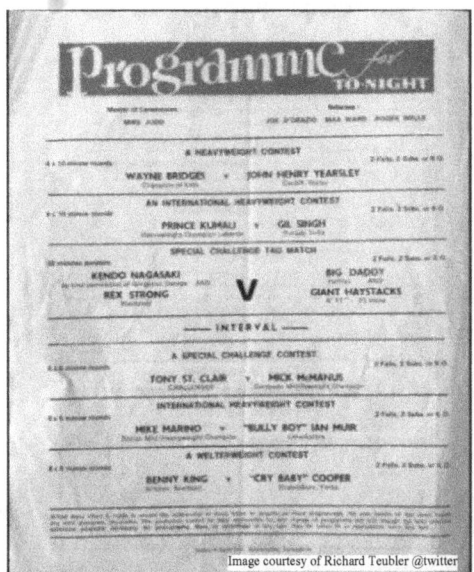

Image courtesy of Richard Teubler @twitter

Tiger Dalbir Gill Singh

Prince Kumali

They enjoyed the programme, while enjoying the snacks and soft drinks during the show.

So we know our boys were smart and travelled in to the city centre and back. They returned back by bus at around 1am in the morning and dropped off Dobir at Wentworth Dwellings and then Altab and Komla walked back home to Reardon house, dropping Komla on the way.

Nothing happened that night and they got home safely.

Altab on the electoral register

```
REARDON HOUSE   E1 9QJ
Reardon Street

1113 Thompson, Margaret        1
1114 Thompson, Samuel          1
1115 Matook, Abdul K.          2
1116 Gachette Maria            3
1117 Gachette, Peter           3
1118 Butler, Alan              4
1119 Gallagher, Josephine      4
1120 Goddard, Sandra A.        5
1121 Schuman, Bernard          5
1122 Begum, Minyra             6
1123 Miah, Badsha              6
1124 Askok, Kuma V.            7
1125 Singh, Gurbachan          7
1126 Surinder, Kaur V.         7
1127 Kaur, Sukhdev             7
1128 Singh, Kashmir            7
1129 Cashman, Julie            8
1130 Cashman, Martin           8
1131 Majid, Amin               8
1132 Abdul, Hussain            9
1133 Altab, Ali                9
1134 Juthsnara, Begum          9
1135 Tovb, Ali                 9
1136 Lake, Eric E.             10
1137 Lake, Joy                 10
1138 Wong, Ma Choi             11
1139 Wong, Poi Ching           11
1140 Corringan, Barbara        12
1141 Corrigan, Denis           12
1142 Jumaid, Mohammed          13
1143 Smith, Irene              13
1144 Lyon, Margaret            14
1145 Lyon, Mary                14
1146 Wallace, Anthony J.       14
1147 Warn, Joseph              15
```

Courtesy of LBTH Archive Library, Bancroft Road, London, E1

We have an image from the electoral archive available at the Tower Hamlets Archive Library 1978-1979. We have documentation that Altab Ali lived at 9 Reardon House with his relatives, and his number was 1133.

Abul Hussain

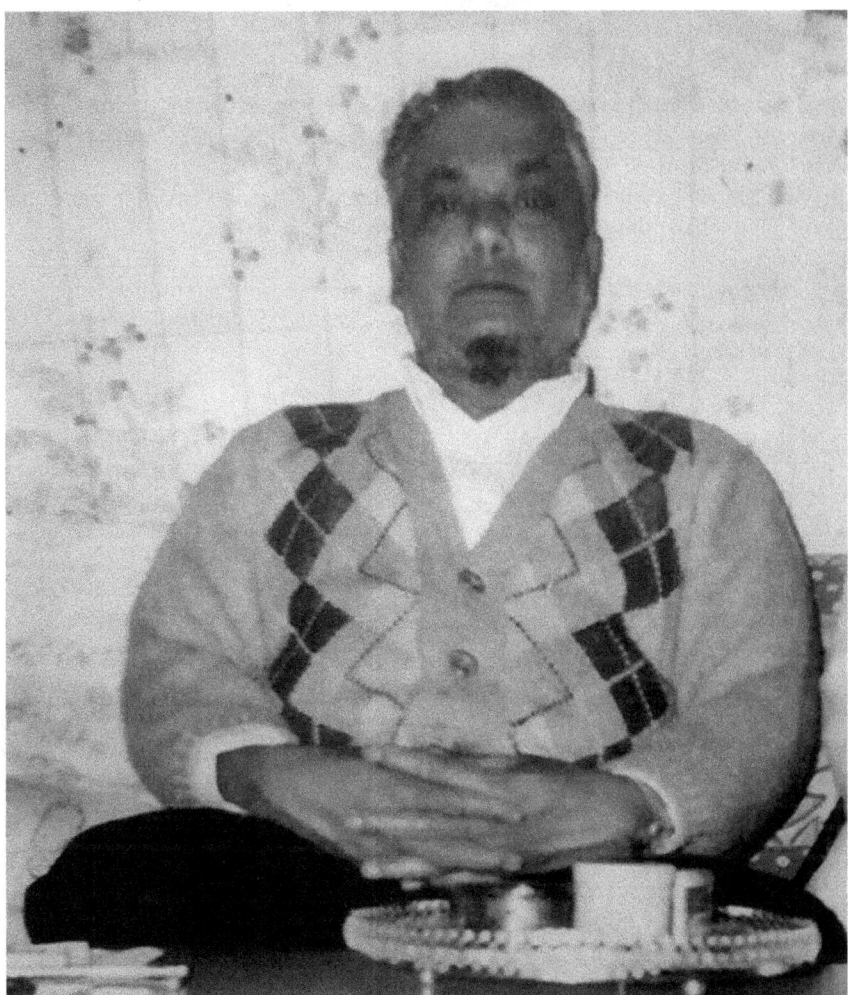

Abul Hussain was Altab's paternal cousin and Altab was Abul's maternal cousin, they were first cousins. Abul was older than him and also came over in UK before him as well as get married before him too.

Abul Hussain brought his wife over and also got himself housed at no. 9 Reardon House. He was pretty much benefiting from the boroughs processes. When they got housed to Wapping they were fearful of the environment as Wapping was notorious for the Bangladeshi community because of the racism in the area from some of the white indigenous hosts.

> "Back in those days a ground floor flat was 'unsafe and vulnerable', quite often the proverbial brick through the window would intimidate a family or worst will inflict serious injury."
>
> Source: Sheik Dobir Miah

So Abul asked Altab to move in with them as a way of feeling and being "safe in numbers." Abul offered the move in as rent free and meals provided, cooked by Abul's wife Jusnara. Altab couldn't turn it down even if he wanted to, he was leaving his very cosy flat with his all male house mates and his roommate, and giving up on his uninhibited life.

> "Altab Ali's relatives like many others at the time felt "safety in numbers" so his cousin asked him to share his family home in the newly acquired council flat"
>
> Source: Sheik Dobir Miah

Abul was his older brother, his first cousin, and taking into account that the Sylheti community are very patriarchal, it would have been very disrespectful and injurious to their relationship if he had refused. According to his roommate Dobir, Altab had a heavy heart and mind to leave the flat. So he had considered his options:

Moving in with his older brother means he will not be free to do and be whatever he wanted to do and to be.

> "However, he will be the nearest to his family that he will ever be.
> He will have his sister-in-law - female member of a family,
> where she will have cooked food and he will stays rent free in the home,"
>
> Source: Sheik Dobir Miah

This means that he leaves his bachelor pad, all men camaraderie's, where male testosterones flared, no inhibitions, stay up and talk about whatever, he was saddened to be leaving the bonds that were formed between each member.

Ultimately even though he didn't have a choice to refuse, the benefits outweighed the move.

There he can have talks about his family openly and candidly with his first cousin and his sister-in-law and other members of the extending family. Their uncle also frequented the flat.

Abul Hussain felt lot more reassured and safer that he had Altab living there who he could trust with his young wife. They can settle in and live a safe and secure living in a hostile borough. There were other Bangladeshi living there and this would have been a bonus for rest of the Bangladeshi families, one more adult man - one more security and a defender.

In the morning of the 4th everything was as normal they had breakfast before they set off to work and his sister-in-law taking her son Anwar to school. Altab and Jusna were making plans for the vote later on as it was the day for the general election. Altab told them to wait for him in the evening and they will go together and vote, and that was the plan.

Later in the early evening Abul returned home from work as per normal casted his vote, and he was hungry and was waiting for his wife to finish cooking. Ever since Altab moved in they all sat together and ate, so Abul's expecting Altab to turn up as per normal, to go and vote and come back and eat. That never happened.

Ever since then Abul was broken and suffered ill health till he died in 2005.

His Family in Bangladesh

Shunaban Bibi

She lost her husband and Altab was her rock, can't imagine her pain and devastation as she was the matriarch of her family. The ground that she stood just disappeared, all security that Altab was has vanished into thin air; not only that, how is she to console her daughter-in-law? The children, the cost, the managing of the event and everything else associated to the death, bereavement and customs and traditions. She died in 2007 in poor state of health; she wouldn't have recovered from losing the first born and their bread winner.

Shitara

Shitara (1963) recollected the moment she learned about her brother's death to her nephew, Akthar Hussain, son of Ukil Ali. Akthar intimated this to me on the 29th February 2020.
On the day of Sunday 7th of May 1978, she went to Altab Ali's wife's village a kilometre away, she was taking over some freshly prepared mango chutney to his mother-in-law, and the mother-in-law was bathing in their front pond.

As Shitara got to pond and handed the chutney over to her and in her hand, news broke out from the house that Altab was dead. Quite clearly, they didn't know that Shitara was there.

It just so happened that while she got there to Altab's mother-in-law; a telegram delivery man arrived from Sylhet town with the news into the main house. One of Altab's in-law family member telegrammed Altab's wife's family.

The telegram was made two day later and Altab had already been dead for two days. The earliest they could send message to the family in Bangladesh. That was the cruel fact, Altab died on Thursday the 4th and the message went Sunday the 7th.

Shitara, upon hearing them words, she didn't stay there, she shot back. That kilometre run, how long was that and the weight of that journey?

Shitara was 15 years of age and Abbas Ali was 8 years of age. Luckily for them their uncle Abdul Hashim was in Bangladesh. This would have been devastating news for him and for Altab's mother. Abdul Hashim would have tried to get in touch with the family in London.

Halima Khatun

Soon after hearing of Altab's death Jahanara [Altab's wife] donated all her dowry gold, her bracelet and other items to the local mosques to pray for him. Jahanara also received 6 acres of land as part of her dowry - 4 acres from his family and 2 acres given by his uncle Abdul Hashim, as Altab was his first nephew, his dearest.

Jahanara returned the land back to them, she did not do away with the land, anything could have happened, but she did what she felt right in her head and heart. This was a noble thing she had done and also she didn't fall victim to bad advice if ever there was any.

This land that Jahanara returned back to the family, the family had split the land up and put to good use. Part of the land was donated to the local mosque which is still standing today.

At our conversation end, Halima drew to her realisation and burst into tears, little did she or they know, that sending him off was going to be the last time they'll see him. See him alive.

Hawarun Nessa

According to Hawarun, Altab's second younger sister, they loved their brother very dearly and that they bore each other's pain instinctively. She doesn't remember details clearly as it has been many years and also she got married and moved away to her husband village. She married Hazi Komor Ali, who passed away 25 years ago now.

She recollects how Altab Ali looked after them, after getting his sisters married he maintained all customs and traditions, the seasonal "Am - Katli" and so on by sending money from London to his mum and then getting the money distributed to them to ensure that all duties are dispensed.

Although her husband has died, her children have fared well, they had 8 children, 4 boys and 4 girls, out of who few of them have gone abroad and have established themselves. She has been fortunate to have had the opportunity to visit the park in 2015, "Altab Ali Park," where her brother was attacked and stabbed; her children were able to take her on a visit.

Unfortunately the other siblings have not had the opportunity to pay homage to their brother's memorial site. It is their familial wish for their younger sister Shitara and brother Abbas Ali to visit. This still hasn't materialised but they are hoping that the organisation's operating under their brother's name to see what they can do.

Newarun

She was the oldest in his sisters and has sadly passed away. I wasn't able to get any information from her, but we know that she was married off after Altab Ali got married and after his body returned back home, her husband was there to support her and the family after they received the devastating news. He was there on the day, received the coffin and would have been in the forefront of supporting the funeral and burial; it is the "done thing", custom and tradition. Newarun would have been devastated.

The women in Altab's family will have been crippled by the news of his death, simply because the new life they transitioned in. They recently spent 6-9 month with their brother, where they were happy, entertained, were complete, the joyous moments, newly-wed, the new in-laws, the familial and societal progress. Altab paying for Newarun's wedding; the second wedding in the family and to further consolidation of the family status; added to their good health.

Ukil Ali

He was the oldest sibling there in Bangladesh with his mum and siblings. He would have been devastated and would have had to man up. He would have had to keep himself together and try and hold everyone and everything together along with his uncle. Fortunately for him he had his uncle Abdul Hashim there, as well as his brother-in-law from his younger sister side, Altab's father-in-law and the family for physical and moral support. How he managed his own grief is not known specifically. Ukil was unable to take an interview, due to his mental health according to his younger brother and his son.

Abbas Ali

Abbas Ali was young at the time but will have remembered who his brother was from the time he had spent at the wedding. He will have further got to have known him through Altab's wife side. He would have been seven and will have witness the grief.

Jahanara Begum

She lost her beloved newly wedded husband, a "tsunami," just wiped everything. All dreams and aspirations, in the honeymoon period of their married life, all those "better," life plans, her social standing and status as a respectable "Londoni bowe," (wife of a Londoner – inference to wealth and resource). The ground that she stood just disappeared too, all security that Altab was has vanished into thin air; not only that; how is she to console her mother-in-law and the children. How was she going to console her own grief and pain, the life devastation she faces, loss of her status as a married woman, she now moves to the "widow," status. This has an altogether different connotation and social standing.

What is cruel for these two women, is that they didn't know that their loved one had been dead for three days and they didn't know and even after being informed of his death, they still had to wait for a month before they can see him; and as a religious custom and tradition, they will not have had a lot of time to see him and be with him, when the body got to them. The body would have been buried as soon as possible; the body was buried the same day.

Bringing his wife over

After returning back to the UK, he had left his wife with his mother in his father's village. There his wife will do the traditional thing to stay with his mother and assist with the family.

She wasn't going to always be staying with her mother in-law, at some point he will bring her over. For him there are many things he would need to sort out such as money, steady income, regular flow of it. A place to stay and I suppose those days it wasn't a social or a community issue to share properties.

As a married man he would be longing for his wife, naturally he would need her; this will have a pull for her and have bearings on him, not to stray or think of going or doing anything immoral, this would keep his mind on a straight path.

Altab in one of his letter asks permission and approval from mother and his guardian uncle Abdul Hashim, if he could start proceedings to get her over here in UK

He then goes on to make arrangement with his father-in-law to facilitate his daughter in obtaining a visa from the British High Commission in Bangladesh. Altab ensures that they do not incur any cost, so he sends money to his wife's dad.

Her first attempt, her interview did not go well and she did not get her visa. That was devastating news for Altab, just would have been a letdown for him as well as leading up to it, an anxious one. To note that there was no mobile phone or internet where you can have instant conversation or give moral support right up till you enter the interview room.

Altab would have waited with baited breath in London on the day.

Altab got to work to get the second attempted and this time he sought his uncles support to facilitate his wife to getting the visa. His uncle was well versed in this matter as he has helped over 35 people to get a visa and come over to UK.

In one of his letter, or particularly the last letter which he wrote on the night of 3.5.1978, which he didn't complete or send it off himself. He was asking his uncle to get involved and help him to get his wife over.

His uncle was not involved from the beginning as he was sidelined by Altab and Jahanara's family. Jahanara's father took the lead then and did not consult his uncle and this was an embarrassment to Abdul Hashim. This is huge problem in a patriarchal society such as in Bangladesh.

Altab had to eat humble pie and lean on his uncle to intervene; clearly his uncle was hurt especially what his uncle did for him and status he stood in the family; there was the element of dishonour and belittling.

This was his final home, resting place.

This was his final resting place, Ukil Ali and Altab's family laid him there. This is how he was until 2017.

Recent discovery

In February 2022 in conversation with Reaz Rahman, the author of "Diary of a Muslim Nobody", mentioned that his uncle Joshim who was around in 1978 and involved with the squatting movement in Pelham building in Deal street, off Hanbury Street, Spitalfields, London

"The Police came and got him from Pelham building to act as an interpreter due to Abul's literacy"

Joshim (who resides in Gants Hill now) declined an interview, so I wasn't able to corroborate this information.

For me learning about this information from Reaz really gave me hope, to get a first hand insight to that evening & the early hours of the morning of 5.5.1978. His account of his time in the police station with Abul Hussain would have given depth, context and also put to rest whether Altab's cousin got arrested or not.

Altab & People

Name	Relationship	Notes
Abbas Ali	Brother	Youngest brother, 7th in line. Family in Bangladesh
Abdul Hashim	Uncle	His paternal uncle was his guardian in UK.
Abdus Samad	Father	Family in Bangladesh
Abul Hussain	Cousin	They were his extended family in UK. Abul was at least 15 years older than Altab Ali
Burhan Uddin	Cousin	He is Altab's cousin, who was with altab Ali in Bangladesh, during the wedding and death times.
Gulam Mostofa	Employer	Employer and from AA's local village who acted as an guardian, GM was also an active community champion.
Jahanara Begum	Wife	AA's Widow, who then returned back to her father and later got her remarried.

Johura Begum		Aunty	Abdul Hashim's wife
Joshim		Public	Interpreter for Abul Hussain at Leman street police station
Jusnara Begum		Sister-in law	Abul Hussain's wife
Kadir Ali		Flatmate	Shared the same flat and amenities, the flat was in his name
Komla Miah (KM)		Friend	Komla is AA's bosom buddy UA1's 1st cousin and AA's friend. AA supported KM during his squatting. AA took KM and Dobir to see wrestling at the Royal Albert Hall, London.
Modoris Ali		Cousin	They were his extended family in UK
Moulovi Emdadur Rahman		Father-in Law	
Sufia Begum		Mother-in-law	
Rohman Ali		Flatmate	Shared the same flat and amenities.
Sheik Dobir Miah		Friend	2nd bosom buddy in absence of Ukil and & Room Mate
Shomor Ali		Flatmate	Shared the same flat and amenities as well as Altab's relation

Shunaban Bibi	Mother	Family in Bangladesh She died in 2008
Suruj Ali	Employer	AA's first employer where he learnt to sew.
Toybur Ali	Cousin	They were his extended family in UK
Toymus Ali	Cousin	They were his extended family in UK
Ukil Ali (UA1)	Friend	His name MA Mohammed Rahman, he was Altab's bosom buddy
Ukil Ali (UAB)	Brother	Younger brother. 4th in line, Family in Bangladesh
Newarun Bibi	Sister	Younger sister, 2nd in line, Family in Bangladesh, She died in 2018.
Hawarun Bibi	Sister	Younger sister 3rd in line, Family in Bangladesh
Kamarun Halima Bibi	Sister	Younger sister 5th in line, Family in Bangladesh

Sheetara Bibi	Sister	Younger sister 6th in line, Family in Bangladesh

Time Line

Date	Description
01-Jan-1910	Altab's father was born (reverse engineered the date)
01-Jan-1914	Altab's uncle, Abdul Hashim was born (reverse engineered)
01-Jan-1932	Abdul Hashim left home, Calcutta bound for work, there was no new about him for the next 13 years. (year is correct but month & day are a filler)
01-Jan-1943	Abdul Hashim sent a letter from London to the family - making contact after 13 years. (year is correct but month & day are a filler)
01-Jan-1947	Abdul Hashim went to Bangladesh, he also built the present mud & tin house, he also saw that his brother got married (Altab's dad) (year is correct but month & day are a filler)
01-Apr-1947	Abdus Samad got married (year is correct but month & day are a filler)
15-Feb-1953	Altab Ali was born (Family)
24 Oct-1953	Altab's DOB in death certificate
03-Jul-1954	Ukil's date of birth
18-Mar-1958	Dobir's date of birth
13-Jun-1958	Jahanara Begum's (Altab's wife) date of birth.
24-Aug-1968	Altab Ali came to UK and lived in Mosley, Birmingham
01-Sept-1968	Ukil arrived in UK
01-Jan-1969	Altab Ali came to UK
05-May-1970	Abbas Ali was born in Bangladesh
01-Jan-1971	Ukil Met Altab at factory
01-Jan-1972	Altab went to learn tailoring at Suruj Ali's & Hussain's factory in Hanbury Street
27-Apr-1972	Altab's father died in Bangladesh of ill health and age, he was around 63 years old.
22-May-1972	Abdul Hashim went to Bangladesh to take over the leading role, he stayed there till 17.8.1978
01-Jun-1974	Altab Ali helped Komla Miah settle in a Squatted place in Everet House.
01-Jul-1974	Ukil & Altab started their petrol pump venture
01-Aug-1974	Ukil & Altab started on the "Bay leaf" business venture
10-Oct-1974	Ukil & Altab get a TV to watch the election results
01-Dec-1974	Altab went to Bangladesh
28-Mar-1975	Altab Ali got married, he married Jahanara Begum.
30-Mar-1975	Altab's Walima, hosted the bride group
01-Jan-1976	Altab returned to London alone.
18-Jan-1976	He wrote a letter and sent it to his family.

01-Jun-1976	He worked in Alley Street, E1, in a Pakistani garment factory, along with Komla Miah, Aptab Miah.
01-Jun-1976	Altab moved into 126 Wentworth Dwellings, E1
01-Jun-1976	Altab worked in Alley Street, E1, in a Pakistani garment factory
01-Jul-1976	Ukil & Altab started their petrol pump venture
12-Jul-1976	Letter received by family dated 12 Jul 1976
01-Aug-1976	He went to Tower Bridge area with friends, Sheik Dobir Miah
17-Aug-1976	Altab wrote letter to his brother Ukil Ali, In Bangladesh
01-Nov-1976	Altab helped Ukil make some Mosquito nets (Moshori) to take home. He always purchased clothes for his family for Ukil to deliver when in Bangladesh.
16-Nov-1976	Ukil went to Bangladesh to get married
01-Jan-1977	Moved to Reardon House (day tbc)
30-Mar-1977	He went to see wrestling at Royal Albert Hall, London, with his friends, Sheik Dobir and Komla Miah.
24-Apr-1977	Ukil got married in Bangladesh
01-Jul-1977	Worked for Gulam Mustafa's garment factory on 54 Hanbury Street.
29-Apr-1978	Saturday - Dobir & Altab had their last encounter, Altab had tea with Dobir at their flat, 126 Wentworth building.
30-Apr-1978	Rock Against Racism - Victoria Park
01-May-1978	National Front Demo to Hoxton Square
04-May-1978	Shishu Choudhury (14) and his uncle Kondokar Alkas Ali were waiting at the bus Stop – Altab collapsed at their feet.
04-May-1978	Murder of Altab Ali
4-May-1978	Impromptu Community meeting was arranged by Toyobur Rahman, Fakuruddin Ahmed where Rofique Ullah and many others were present – addressing the murder of Altab Ali.
05-May-1978	Altab Ali's cousin Abul Hussain was released and dropped off home at around 4am in the morning.
05-May-1978	Joshim – was collected from Pelham Building by the Lemen Street Police to translate and interpret for them with Abul Hussain in the early hours.
06-May-1978	Murder sign put up
06-May-1978	First paper article - The Daily mail - run a 25 word article about Altab's Murder
06-May-1978	Murder poster created
07-May-1978	Meeting took place at the Grand Palais Cinema hall. 78 hours after the murder of Altab Ali.
7-May-1978	Telegram was sent to Bangladesh, to Altab's father in law.
09-May-1978	Sketch of the murderers faces
11-May-1978	East Enders Article -

12-May-1978	Times article - with the Artist impressions of the attackers
14-May-1978	Demo - taking the coffin to Hyde Park & Downing Street. The coffin was empty, there was no body, body was not released, and it was still at the coroners.
14-May-1978	Seven designated persons hand delivered the petition to 10 Downing Street
15-May-1978	Times article
26-May-1978	Evening standards article
01-Jun-1978	Body was released
02-Jun-1978	Friday Jamat Janaza - Funeral Prayers performed
02-Jun-1978	Bangladesh High Commissioner H.E. Aminur Rahman Shamsud Doha, attended Altab Ali's Janaza at East London Mosque
03-Jun-1978	Body boarded the plane to Bangladesh
04-Jun-1978	Ukil help bury Altab's body in Bangladesh
04-Jun-1978	Altab's dead body was received by his family in Bangladesh, and buried after a funeral prayer same day.
28 Jun-1978	The killers were arrested
04-Jul-1978	Ukil returned back to UK
07-Jul-1978	Murderer remanded in custody until sentencing
11-Jul 1978	Death Registration
16-Jul-1978	Inquest
17-Jul-1978	Rampage - 200 White Youths rampaged in Brick Lane.
05-Aug-1978	Times Article
17-Aug-1978	Abdul Hashim returned back to UK, to sort his paper work out, for pension and etc.
20-Aug-1978	Brick Lane Demo by Tower Hamlets Defence Committee & Anti Nazi League
22-Nov-1978	Sentence @ the Old Bailey
01-Jan-1979	His paternal uncle Abdul Hashim died in the London Hospital
30-Jun-1979	Times article
01-Oct-1989	The Altab Ali arch was unveiled, created by David Peterson.
04-May-1994	The Park was dedicated to the memory of Altab Ali
04-May-1998	Name change to the park
01-Jan-2005	Altab's cousin - (Fufuto bai) Abul Hussain died this year,
02-May 2010	Whitechapel Anarchist Group – commemorate Altab Ali Day with Mohammed Haque & Shams Uddin in Altab Ali park.
04-May-2010	Altab Ali Foundation set up
01-Jul-2014	Md Jubair - Channel S reporter - Met with Altab's family in Bangladesh and acquired some original document of Altab Ali - such as Altab's diary and other documents. The family did not have any back up.

31-Dec-2014	Jahanara's father Moulovi Emdadul Rahman passed away.
1-Apr-2012	Mayor Lutfur Rahman improves Altab Ali park
01-Oct-2015	Mayor John Biggs: LBTH Announced hosting of annual commemoration of Altab Ali Day
01-Jan-2016	Altab Ali Trust was set up
06-May-2017	Shishu – commented on Mohammed Ahmedullah's blogs – regarding witnessing Altab Ali's demise and how that has affected him. *https://www.imbuenomad.com/when-I-was-attacked-in-green-street-at-1-30-am-in-1977/*.
11-Jul-2018	Cllr Puru Miah, Bus stop name change issue was raised in the LBTH council chambers meeting.
14-Oct-2018	Candle lit vigil for Altab Ali and Stephen Lawrence at St Paul's Cathedral, London.
29-Oct-2018	Unmesh Desai: (TFL) Transport for London confirmed that the Alder Street Bus stop in Whitechapel will be renamed to "Altab Ali"
31-Oct-2018	Bus stop name change
05-Oct-2019	Mayar Akash wrote "High Forever"
31-Jan-2020	Mayar Akash had a brief conversation with Jusna, Abul Hussain's widow.
17-Feb-2020	Altab's grave was officiated by Rafique Ullah and accompanied by Abdal Ullah in Bangladesh at Altab's village.
27-Apr-2021	Waheed-ul-Raza Choudhury a.k.a. Shishu Choudhury – sent me photo of himself from the that time in 1978. How he looked then.
11-Feb 2023	King Charles III & the Queen Consort Camilla visited Altab Ali park and the King planted a tree there, a tree that the King chose. This event was put together by Abdal Ullah and his wife, Ayesha Quraishi MBE, as part of their organisation BBPI – British Bangladeshi Power - Inspiration

Glossary

Transliteration in Sylheti dialect of Bangladesh.

Words	Meaning/Description
Amm	Mango
Amm Khatli	Tradition & Custom of taking mango and jackfruit to your sister's in-law – beginning of the season.
Badsha	King
Bahbee	Sister-in-law
Bai	Brother
Baira	Brother in law
Baul	Devotional singing about Islam
Bdt	Bangladesh Taka
Belati	Foreigner
Bowe	Daughter-in-law
Elamer Gaon	Location name
Fandan	Beetle nut tray
Fandangry	Possessive and authoritative over the Beetle nut tray
Fandanology	Knowing everything about the Beetle nut and & Pan
Fufu	Paternal Aunt
Fufu To Bai	Cousin from Paternal Aunt side
Jumma	Friday prayer
Katli	Jack Fruit
Komla	Orange
Koybor	Grave
Londoni Bowe	Daughter-in-law from London
Moshori	Mosquito net
Moulovi	a learned teacher of Islamic law
Mulla-Ata	Location name
Pubali	Name Of A Bank In Bangladesh
Rajakars	Pro-west Pakistan supporter
Shahid Minar	Martyrs Monument
Taka	Name Of The Bangladeshi Money / Currency
Toki Pur	Location name
Walima	Tradition and Custom – Groom side return the wedding feast for the bride side.
Ziaroth	Prayer Of Commemoration

Bibliography

Uddin, Nobab, East London 1978, The Racist Murder of Altab Ali, resistance to Racism, (Dhaka, Bangladesh, Ittadi Grantha Prokash, February 2020)

Faruk, Bakth, Shahagir, Brick Lane, Bari to Basha, (UK, Lightning Source UK)

Glynn, Sarah, Class, Ethnicity and Religion in the Bengali East End, A Political History (Manchester University Press, 2017)

Leech, Kenneth, Brick Lane 1978, The events and their significance, (revised 1994)

Uddin, Nobab, Mohammed, Racist Murder of Altab Ali (Dhaka, Bangladesh, Ittadi Grantha Prokash, February 2019)

Forrester, Cathy, Remembering the 70s (Altab Ali Foundation website, 2019)

Uddin, Jalal, Rajon, Remembering the 70s (Altab Ali Foundation website, 2019)

Hasan, Jamal, , Remembering the 70s (Altab Ali Foundation website, 2019)

Lutfa, Renu, Article in Nobab Uddins book, Racist Murder of Altab Ali (Dhaka, Bangladesh, Ittadi Grantha Prokash, February 2019)

Source/References

1. bbc.co.uk
2. http://www.wikiwand.com/en/British_Bangladeshi#/History[7.2.19]
3. http://thestirrer.thebirminghampress.com/blair-peach-the-road-to-southall-0404091.html[7.2.19]
4. https://pasttenseblog.wordpress.com/2016/05/14/today-in-londons-radical-history-7000-march-behind-racist-murder-victim-altab-alis-coffin-to-downing-st-1978/[7.2.19]
5. https://alchetron.com/Altab-Ali[7.2.19]
6. https://www.timeout.com/london/news/the-fight-still-isnt-over-remembering-the-battle-of-brick-lane-40-years-on-[27.7.18]
7. https://www.bbc.co.uk/news/av/stories-45877154/how-a-racist-murder-mobilised-britain-s-bengali-community[1-10-19]
8. https://kenanmalik.com/2018/05/05/altab-ali-and-brick-lane-1978/[1-10-19]
9. https://www.opendemocracy.net/en/shine-a-light/remembering-altab-ali/[1.10.19]
10. http://www.worldwrite.org.uk/londonbehindthescenes/bricklane/altabalipark.html[1.10.19]
11. https://historicengland.org.uk/research/inclusive-heritage/another-england/your-stories/altab-ali-park/[8-10-19]
12. https://www.discoveringbritain.org/activities/greater-london/walks/bengali-east-end.html[9-10-19]
13. http://www.towerhamletsarts.org.uk/?cid=63602&guide=Venues[6-10-19]
14. https://www.eastlondonadvertiser.co.uk/news/heritage/altab-ali-s-whitechapel-murder-protest-march-depicted-in-four-corners-radical-archive-launch-of-1970s-life-1-5572501[6-10-19]
15. https://www.spacehive.com/thealtabalistory[7-10-19]
16. http://www.mukulandghettotigers.com/altab-ali-story/[7-10-19]
17. http://purumiah.com/responding-to-rod-liddle-in-tower-hamlets-need-to-be-tough-on-racism-but-also-tough-on-the-root-causes-of-racism/[7-10-19]
18. https://journeytojustice.org.uk/projects/tower-hamlets/[9-10-19]
19. http://iupss.com/remembering-altab-ali-exhibition-including-work-from-macarena-bonhomme/
20. [2.12.19]
21. https://rlqns.com/2018/03/15/the-history-of-neurosurgery-at-the-royal-london-hospital/[2.12.19]
22. https://www.london.gov.uk/press-releases/assembly/unmesh-desai/altab-ali-commemorated-with-bus-stop-name-change[2.12.19]
23. https://www.britishnewspaperarchive.co.uk/viewer/BL/0000560/19780506/046/0006?browse=true[4.12.19]
24. https://www.theguardian.com/music/2008/apr/20/popandrock.race[4.12.19]

25. https://en.wikipedia.org/w/index.php?search=liberation+flag+of+banglades h&title=Special:Search&go=Go&ns0=1[5.12.19]
26. https://www.zoopla.co.uk/for-sale/details/52645998[5.12.19] (picture of Reardon house)
27. http://www.londoni.co/index.php/23-history-of-bangladesh/1971-muktijuddho/127-muktijuddho-bangladesh-liberation-war-1971-uk-mission-usa-mission-history-of-bangladesh[5.12.19]
28. https://www.liberationwarmuseumbd.org/photo-gallery/[5.12.19]
29. http://banglamirrornews.com/2018/10/17/vigil-at-st-pauls-altab-ali-remembered/[5.12.19]
30. https://www.facebook.com/pg/Tower-Hamlets-1636786886607724/photos/?tab=album&album_id=1646148339004912[10.12.19]
31. http://www.ukrockfestivals.com/victoria-park-1978.html?fbclid=IwAR2i2fAVcuGnRcptpyHn6emuaiU_oOGXrHpqH0vpYe7nc2jRYhNugb62NgY[10.12.19]
32. A. K Azad Konor, The Battle of brick lane 1978, Grosvenor House Publishing Ltd, 2018 (p29)
33. https://www.casebook.org/forum/messages/4923/18937.html[16.12.19]
34. www.horoscope.co[20.12.2019]
35. https://www.youtube.com/watch?v=LRKlDBhAOi8[24.12.19]
36. http://britishsubjects.annaro.se/2019/04/30/18-52-bangladesh-altab-ali/[24.12.19]
37. https://www.purumiah.com/summer-thoughts-2-remembering-the-summer-of-1978-the-murder-of-altab-ali-and-the-unfinished-revolution/[24.12.19]
38. https://kenanmalik.com/2018/05/05/altab-ali-and-brick-lane-1978/[24.12.19]
39. https://www.opendemocracy.net/en/shine-a-light/remembering-altab-ali/[24.12.19]
40. https://www.youtube.com/watch?v=gj-CTFQrDDw[27.12.19]
41. https://khoodeelaar.wordpress.com/2012/08/23/altab-ali-memorial-gives-two-different-years-when-he-was-murdered/[28.12.19]
42. https://www.youtube.com/watch?v=8S-ALefdq1E[28.12.19]
43. https://www.cagematch.net/?id=2&nr=218&page=4[30.12.19]
44. https://twitter.com/rteubler[31.12.19]
45. https://medium.com/bangladeshiidentity/forty-years-on-how-the-murder-of-altab-ali-mobilized-bangladeshis-in-londons-east-end-e48b9d419ac5[1.1.2020]
46. http://gilburtandpaul.co.uk/index.php/notebook-2/[1.1.2020]
47. https://twitter.com/mayorjohnbiggs/status/860454795047563264[3.1.2020]
48. http://shottobani.com/2017/05/23/altab-ali-place-history/[3.1.2020]
49. https://www.londonremembers.com/memorials/st-mary-matfelon[4.1.2020]
50. http://muf.co.uk/portfolio/altab-ali-park/[4.1.2020]
51. https://maryamnamazie.com/todays-altab-ali-day-2013/

52. https://web.archive.org/web/20140419020307/http://www.runnymedetrust.org/histories/race-equality/71/altab-ali-murdered-in-whitechapel-london.html[7-1-2020]
53. https://www.cobosocial.com/dossiers/rasheed-araeen-and-his-performance-art/[7-1-2020]
54. https://cargocollective.com/akvile-terminaite/Poetic-East-End[7-1-2020]
55. https://www.eastlondonlines.co.uk/2016/05/bengali-community-remembers-altab-alis-murder-through-new-play/[7-1-2020]
56. http://the-radical-truth.blogspot.com/2012/05/altab-ali-day-and-history-of-bengali.html[7-1-2020]
57. http://sielle.co.uk/altab-ali/4561680480[7-1-2020]
58. http://londonlandscapeobservatory.blogspot.com/2012/03/click-here-for-photos-ltab-ali-park-has.html[7-1-2020]
59. https://www.thetimes.co.uk/archive/article/1978-05-02/2/10.html#start%3D1978-05-01%26end%3D1978-12-31%26terms%3Ddemonstrations%20East%20End%20of%20London%26back%3D/tto/archive/find/demonstrations+East+End+of+London/w:1978-05-01%7E1978-12-31/1%26prev%3D/tto/archive/frame/goto/demonstrations+East+End+of+London/w:1978-05-01%7E1978-12-31/7%26next%3D/tto/archive/frame/goto/demonstrations+East+End+of+London/w:1978-05-01%7E1978-12-31/9[21-10-2020]
60. http://www.election.demon.co.uk/thbc/summary.html[21-1-2020]
61. https://www.britishnewspaperarchive.co.uk/viewer/bl/0000560/19781123/032/0007[21-1-2020]
62. https://player.bfi.org.uk/free/film/watch-credo-1978-online[22-1-2020]
63. http://www.altabalifoundation.org.uk/articles/Remembering_The_1970s(CF[P]).pdf[23-1-2020]
64. https://www.google.com/search?client=firefox-b-d&q=old+bailey+visit&sa=X&ved=2ahUKEwjHs_iBnarnAhUNYsAKHQzAAZIQ1QIoB3oECAsQCA&biw=1920&bih=966[30-1-2020]
65. https://www.revolvy.com/page/Basil-Wigoder?cr=1[30-1-2020]
66. https://en.wikipedia.org/wiki/Basil_Wigoder[30-1-2020]
67. https://www.youtube.com/watch?v=ZkrlLV9OZIA[4-2-2020]
68. https://www.gettyimages.co.uk/detail/video/camera-london-brick-lane-deputy-assistant-commissioner-news-footage/1151141586?adppopup=true[22-2-2020]
69. https://www.youtube.com/watch?v=Pkoy3JdNgoA&t=7s[22-2-2020]
70. https://www.youtube.com/watch?v=LIACI_MwMOs&t=2825s[26-2-2020]
71. https://www.google.com/search?client=firefox-b-d&q=when+was+mujib+assasinated%3F[01.03.2020]
72. https://whitechapelanarchistgroup.wordpress.com/2010/04/07/remember-altab-ali-may-2nd/?unapproved=9603&moderation-hash=149f3c26e740f4dccc331614e63b008c#comment-9603[26-3-2020]

73. https://fxtop.com/en/historical-currency-converter.php?A=8000&C1=GBP&C2=BDT&DD=01&MM=06&YYYY=1979&B=1&P=&I=1&btnOK=Go%21[12-5-2020]
74. https://bengalicalendar.com/index.php?year=1425&month=Kartik[6-4-2020]
75. http://www.onlineworldofwrestling.com/profile/prince-kumali/[24-7-2020]
76. https://shop.royalalberthall.com/collections/sport/products/pod1032773[24-7-2020]
77. https://www.ewrestlingnews.com/articles/the-best-of-british-vol-9-big-daddy-vs-giant-haystacks[24-7-2020]
78. https://twitter.com/memorialdevice/status/1225720129046052864[24-7-2020]
79. https://www.theguardian.com/commentisfree/belief/2012/apr/17/pakistan-goodbye-allah-hafiz[24-7-2020]
80. https://hprints.com/en/search/Alfred-Dunhill-Cigarettes-Tobacco-Smoking/[24-8-2020]
81. https://purpleart.hk/docs/lou-thesz-vs-dara-singh-266bd2[30.10.2020]
82. https://www.wrestlingheritage.co.uk/tony-scarlo[30.10.2020]

MAPublisher Catalogue

ISBN/Titles /Image/Author	ISBN/Titles /Image/Author	ISBN/Titles /Image/Author	ISBN/Titles /Image/Author
978-1-910499-00-9 Father to child By Mayar Akash	978-1-910499-08-5 HSJ Lakri Tura By Mayar Akash	978-1-910499-26-9 Colouring 1-10 By MAPublisher	978-1-910499-18-4 Basic Numbers 1-10 By MAPublisher
978-1-910499-16-0 River of Life By Mayar Akash	978-1-910499-09-2 HSJ Gilaf Procession By Mayar Akash	978-1-910499-27-6 Activity Numbers 1-10 By MAPublisher	978-1-910499-19-1 Number 1-100 By MAPublisher
978-1-910499-39-9 Eyewithin By Mayar Akash	978-1-910499-03-0 HSJ Mazar Sharif By Mayar Akash	978-1-910499-28-3 Activity Colouring Alphabets By MAPublisher	978-1-910499-20-7 Vowels By MAPublisher
978-1-910499-32-0 WG Survivor By Mayar Akash	978-1-910499-06-1 Hazrat Shahjalal By Mayar Akash	978-1-910499-68-9 The Adventures of Sylheti mazars By Mayar Akash	978-1-910499-21-4 Alphabet Consonants By MAPublisher
978-1-910499-66-5 Yesteryears By Mayar Akash	978-1-910499-07-8 HSJ Urus By Mayar Akash	978-1-910499-38-2 Bite Size Islam: 99 Names of Allah By Mayar Akash	978-1-910499-22-1 Vowels & Short By MAPublisher

ISBN/Titles /Image/Author	ISBN/Titles /Image/Author	ISBN/Titles /Image/Author	ISBN/Titles /Image/Author
978-1-910499-15-3 Anthology One By Penny Authors	978-1-910499-36-8 Delirious By Liam Newton	978-1-910499-52-8 Lit From Within By Ruth Lewarne	978-1-910499-57-3 The Vampire of the Resistance By Ruth Lewarne
978-1-910499-17-7 Anthology Two By Penny Authors	978-1-910499-54-2 Book of Lived v6 Penny Authors	978-1-910499-49-8 Cry for Help By B. M. Gandhi	978-1-910499-55-9 Riversolde By Meriyon
978-1-910499-29-0 Book of Lived v3 By Penny Authors	978-1-910499-37-5 When You Look Back By Rashma Mehta	978-1-910499-14-6 The Halloweeen Poem by Zainab Khan	978-1-910499-70-2 Smiley & The Acorn By Roger Underwood
978-1-910499-351 V4 Book of Lived By Penny Authors	978-1-910499-37-5 My Dream World By Rashma Mehta	978-1-910499-69-6 Consciousness By Mustak Mustafa	978-1-910499-40-5 World's First University By Giasuddin Ahmed
978-1-910499-50-4 Book of Lived v5 By Penny Authors	978-1-910499-53-5 Angel Eyez By Rashma Mehta	978-1-910499-73-3 Book of Lived v7 By Penny Authors	978-1-910499-56-6 The Warrior Queen By Giasuddin Ahmed

All books are available on-line, Google the titles and they will take you to the sites where you can acquire copies.

ISBN/Titles /Image/Author	ISBN/Titles /Image/Author	ISBN/Titles /Image/Author	ISBN/Titles /Image/Author
978-1-910499-58-0 EEP:Tower Hamlets, Random, One Mayar Akash	978-1-910499-60-3 EEP:Tower Hamlets, Random, Two By Mayar Akash	978-1-910499-05-4 Tide of Change By Mayar Akash	978-1-910499-51-1 Brick & Mortar By Mayar Akash
978-1-910499-61-0 Grenfell Tower By Mayar Akash	978-1-910499-63-4 EEP: Power Houses, Clove Crescent By Mayar Akash	978-1-910499-71-9 Altab Ali Murder By Mayar Akash	978-1-910499-31-3 Pathfinders By Mayar Akash
978-1-910499-62-7 EEP: Community Service 1992-1993 By Mayar Akash	978-1-910499-64-1 EEP:Bancroft Estate By Mayar Akash	978-1-910499-11-5 Re-Awakening By Mayar Akash	978-1-910499-13-9 Chronicle of Sylhetis of UK By Mayar Akash
978-1-910499-59-7 EEP:Brick Lane, Spitalfields By Mayar Akash	978-1-910499-72-6 25th Anniversary of Bangladesh By Mayar Akash	978-1-910499-12-2 Young Voice Mayar Akash	978-1-910499-42-9 Bangladeshi Fishes By Mayar Akash
978-1-910499-65-8 PYO Polish Exchange 1992 By Mayar Akash	978-1-910499-30-6 TH Bangladeshi Politicians By Mayar Akash	978-1-910499-10-8 Vigil Subotaged By Mayar Akash	978-1-910499-67-2 F. Ahmed and History By Mukid Choudhury

All books are available on-line, Google the titles and they will take you to the sites where you can acquire copies.

ISBN/Titles /Image/Author	ISBN/Titles /Image/Author	ISBN/Titles /Image/Author	ISBN/Titles /Image/Author
978-1-910499-43-6 My Life Book 1 By Mayar Akash	978-1-910499-44-3 My Life Book 2 By Mayar Akash	978-1-910499-45-0 My Life Book 3 By Mayar Akash	978-1-910499-46-7 My Life Book 4 By Mayar Akash
978-1-910499-47-4 My Life Book 5 By Mayar Akash	978-1-910499-75-7 Bangladeshis in Manchester - Oral History, Part 1 By M.A. Mustak	978-1-910499-74-0 Peter Fox Artist By Peter Fox	978-1-910499-78-8 On The Seventh Day By Cosette Ratliff

All books are available on-line, Google the titles and they will take you to the sites where you can acquire copies.

www.mapublisher.org.uk